THE
EVERYTHING®
BIG BOOK
OF JOKES

Dear Reader,

An early childhood memory of mine involves the morning bus to school. While other kids were getting a couple of extra minutes of sleep, starting homework that was due that day, or gazing out the window at the passing scenes, I spent the time catching up on reading. But I wasn't cracking open textbooks; I was cracking myself up with the latest *Mad* magazine or one-dollar joke book from the neighborhood drug store.

One morning, after chuckling a little too loudly at a joke—which ironically was about school—an older student stuck his head over my seat and asked what was so funny. I read him the joke and he laughed just as loud. By the time the bus pulled into the school parking lot, I had most of the students rolling in the aisles at the jokes, one-liners, and gags. Even though the source material did all of the work, I still reaped the benefits. It was at that moment I realized the power of humor.

Not everyone possesses the gift to craft a joke or the wit to execute a solid pun, but it's a learned skill. My hope is that this book inspires people to inject more humor in their lives.

Just remember: "Laugh and the world laughs with you."—Ella Wheeler Wilcox

Best,

Evan C. Thomas

Welcome to the EVERYTHING® Series!

These handy, accessible books give you all you need to tackle a difficult project, gain a new hobby, or even brush up on something you learned back in school but have since forgotten. You can choose to read from cover to cover or just pick out information from our four useful boxes.

 Famous Funnies

Quotes from Popular Comics

 Comedy Facts

Important Snippets of Information

 Joke Essentials

Tips and Advice

 Ask the Comedian

Answers to Common Questions

When you're done reading, you can finally say you know **EVERYTHING®**!

PUBLISHER Karen Cooper

MANAGING EDITOR, EVERYTHING® SERIES Lisa Laing

COPY CHIEF Casey Ebert

ASSISTANT PRODUCTION EDITOR Alex Guarco

ACQUISITIONS EDITOR Lisa Laing

ASSOCIATE DEVELOPMENT EDITOR Eileen Mullan

EVERYTHING® SERIES COVER DESIGNER Erin Alexander

Visit the entire Everything® series at *www.everything.com*

THE
EVERYTHING®
BIG BOOK OF JOKES

Hundreds of the shortest,
longest, silliest, smartest, most
hilarious jokes you've never heard!

Evan C. Thomas

Adams Media
New York London Toronto Sydney New Delhi

This book is dedicated to all of the people who have ever made me laugh. Especially my wife and kids, who make me laugh harder and love more than I ever thought possible.

Adams Media
An Imprint of Simon & Schuster, Inc.
57 Littlefield Street
Avon, Massachusetts 02322

An Everything® Series Book.
Everything® and everything.com® are registered trademarks of Simon & Schuster, Inc.

ADAMS MEDIA and colophon are trademarks of Simon and Schuster.

For information about special discounts for bulk purchases, please contact Simon & Schuster Special Sales at 1-866-506-1949 or business@simonandschuster.com.

The Simon & Schuster Speakers Bureau can bring authors to your live event. For more information or to book an event contact the Simon & Schuster Speakers Bureau at 1-866-248-3049 or visit our website at www.simonspeakers.com.

Manufactured in the United States of America

10 9 8

Library of Congress Cataloging-in-Publication Data has been applied for.

ISBN 978-1-4405-7697-3
ISBN 978-1-4405-7698-0 (ebook)

Acknowledgments

I'd like to thank Lisa Laing, Eileen Mullan, and everyone at Adams Media. My literary agent, Grace Freedson, and my family, friends, and anyone who has ever told me a joke.

Contents

Top 10 Reasons Why Everyone Needs to Laugh More Often

1. Laughter increases HGH (Human Growth Hormone). Research has shown that even the anticipation of a good laugh produces as much as an 87 percent increase in HGH in the body. HGH is an anti-aging hormone.

2. Laughter boosts the immune system. According to the National Cancer Institute, laughing keeps stress hormones under control.

3. Humor is a coping mechanism. Laughter not only helps with stressful situations, but releases endorphins in the brain to help a person deal with tragedy, personal loss, and depression.

4. Laughter promotes learning. Think back to your days in school. Did you learn more from strict teachers or from teachers who used humor in their lessons?

5. Humor eases tense situations. If used properly, humor can diffuse a potentially volatile situation. If you find yourself in a tight spot, humor can get you out safely.

6. Laughter is a universal language. Even though people speak different languages, a smile or laugh is understood by any culture or creed.

7. Humor shows intellect. Not everyone is capable of crafting a good joke. In all honesty, some people can't even memorize a joke.

8. Laughter improves relationships. Research shows that families who laugh together have a closer bond, and couples who can make each other laugh stay together longer.

9. It makes you more attractive. The ability to laugh, and make others laugh, is one of the more attractive attributes in a friend or potential spouse.

10. It improves self-opinion. The most important opinion in your life is your own, and feeling good about yourself is the key to a long, healthy life.

Introduction

According to the ancient adage, laughter is the best medicine. Everyone wants to laugh, and everyone wants to make other people laugh. It's the reason people spend money to see a funny movie or visit a local comedy club.

Laughter is a universal language. It's possible for people from completely different backgrounds, cultures, upbringings, and religions to find the same joke, gag, or pun funny. Humor is a bonding experience. Laughter brings people together and breaks down all barriers.

These are all very valid reasons to tell jokes. If you want to be the person who makes people laugh, you should aspire to be constantly armed with a one-liner, quip, wisecrack, or yarn. Orny Adams, a stand-up comic and actor, once said, "I never even knew pain until I got into comedy."

Being funny is a tough business. If you're telling an original joke, retelling a classic, or just trying to lighten the mood, joke telling is a risky proposition. For every joke that lands, there are hundreds more that fall with a thud.

A good comedian knows when to tell a joke, but almost as important, knows when not to tell a joke. The industry term is "knowing the audience." If the joke is about something complicated or is inappropriate for some ages, be careful with your choice. Examine the mood of the audience. Are they ready to laugh at a joke? Is it really the situation to make a joke? Obviously, the answer should be "yes" to both.

Knowing your surroundings is as important as knowing the audience. It's best to think of every joke as a miniature story. To tell your story, and to get the best reaction (in this case a laugh), you will want the undivided attention of the audience. If the social situation involves audience members floating in and out of the group or constant interruptions from sources outside the group, it might not be the best time to tell the joke. The size of the audience is also a factor. Telling a joke to a group of more than four gets harder with the more listeners added to the group. If the group is larger than ten, grab a mic, because you might as well be in a comedy club.

If the time is right, and you've got a joke in mind, never ask for permission to tell a joke. Surprise is crucial in joke telling. Asking permission is equal to saying, "I'm about to say something funny so get ready to laugh," which usually kills a joke right out of the gate.

Jokes are the great equalizer, and strong is the man or woman equipped with a robust repertoire to amuse the masses. That's just a fancy way of saying that if you've got a ton of jokes at your disposal, people will really like you. Luckily for you, this book has a ton of jokes.

CHAPTER 1

The Who, What, Where, and How of Jokes

The first joke dates back to Adam and Eve, to the moment right after Eve told Adam she'd bitten into the forbidden apple. Adam looked at Eve and said, "Are you joking?" Comedy has come a long way over the years, but the major goal has always been the same: to make people laugh.

A Brief History of Jokes

Actually, the world's oldest joke dates back to 1900 B.C., according to a list published by the University of Wolverhampton in 2008. The joke was more of an expression than anything else, but it was popular with the Sumerians, a group of people who resided in the area now known as southern Iraq. The Sumerian joke translated into English says: "Something which has never occurred since time immemorial; a young woman did not fart in her husband's lap."

That's right—the world's oldest joke is about farts.

The oldest British joke dates back to the tenth century A.D. and is incredibly naughty for its time. The joke goes, "What hangs at a man's thigh and wants to poke the hole that it's often poked before?"

"A key."

Comedy Facts

The idea of comedy, or making people laugh, has origins in ancient Greek street performers and masked performers that were popular in sixteenth-century Italy. Historians also point to the female comedic roles in Shakespeare's plays as an origin of the modern-day jokes. It should be noted that in the earliest Shakespearean performances, men played the roles of women, so the real joke came when the performers took off their dresses at the after party.

 # Famous Funnies

"Two babies were born on the same day at the same hospital. They lay there and looked at each other. Their families took them home the next day. Eighty years later, by a bizarre coincidence, they lay in the same hospital again, on their deathbeds, right next to each other. One man looked at the other and said, 'So, what did you think?'"—Stephen Wright

A document dating back to the fourth century A.D., titled *Philogelos* (which translates to "The Laughter Lover"), written by Hierocles and Philagrius, contains more than two hundred jokes. Apparently Hierocles and Philagrius went on to tour the world as a successful comedy team known as Hiero and Phil. When the duo split up, each man took a hundred jokes, but never found much success.

Different Types of Humor

There are several different kinds of humor, most of which are probably already familiar to you.

Slapstick

Slapstick humor relies very heavily on physicality. Examples of slapstick humor include Charlie Chaplin, the Three Stooges, and early Jim Carrey (in case you were born after 1984 and you don't know who the heck those other people are). Slapstick often relies on the absurd moments in life. Though jokes aren't really considered slapstick—you won't be smacking anyone as a punch line—the actual telling of a joke can rely on the physical. A facial expression, gesture, or even a fake fall can accentuate the punch line.

 Famous Funnies

"Our bombs are smarter than the average high school student. At least they can find Kuwait."—A. Whitney Brown

Sarcasm

Sarcasm can be seen in an ironic or satirical remark. When using sarcasm, it may seem that you are praising a person or thing, but the remark is actually taunting or cutting in its intent. Sarcasm is biting and usually dark. Political cartoons, the stand-up comedy of Daniel Tosh, and anything Bill Murray has ever done or said are perfect examples of well-executed sarcasm.

"I feel so miserable without you, it's almost like having you here." —Stephen Bishop

Satire

Satire is a joke style that playfully ridicules or criticizes the subject as an attempt to bring about change. Satire is an effective means to poke fun at individuals, ideals, institutions, and any subject that is usually off limits. When done correctly, satire can be used to make a point without being blunt. *The Daily Show* and *Colbert Report* are satire at its finest.

"Girlfriend Overdoses on Lotion" —headline on the *Onion*, January 2014

Self-Deprecating

A popular type of humor, and probably the safest, self-deprecation is making yourself the butt of the joke. It's the act of belittling or undervaluing yourself in an effort to make others laugh or just feel better about their own shortcomings. While self-deprecating humor is intended to make others laugh, there is a fine line between joking about yourself and being too hard on yourself. Knocking yourself down for the amusement of others isn't always the best way to go through life. Mike Birbiglia is a hilarious and successful comedian who relies heavily on self-deprecating humor, but knows how to dish it out in small doses.

"I'm not the kind of guy who has a huge weight problem, but I am the kind of guy who could really put the brakes on an orgy. Everyone would be like, 'Was he invited? Why is he eating a cake?' I've never been in an orgy. I feel like it'd be like what happens when I try and play pick-up basketball. Like, no one passes me the ball; everyone asks me to keep my shirt on." —Mike Birbiglia

Toilet Humor

Perhaps the most beloved type of humor, especially since the world's oldest joke is about a fart, toilet humor appeals to the lowest common denominator. Toilet humor is joking about the use of bodily functions to get a laugh. These are the jokes and gags that are off-color, gross, offensive to most, and best when told in hushed tones and to specific groups. Though this humor is designed for the perverted and perverse parts of our brain, the one thing that toilet humor has over others is that anyone can "get" bathroom humor. While satire, self-deprecation, and sarcasm often go over the heads of some, everyone "gets" a poop joke. They might not laugh, but they get it. The *Jackass* movies are proof that toilet humor can be incredibly lucrative.

> *"You don't have to be smart to laugh at farts, but you have to be stupid not to."* —Louis CK

Highbrow Humor

Highbrow humor is the polar opposite of toilet humor. It is intended for sophisticated audiences. Basically, they are jokes only "smarter" people will understand. These jokes rely heavily on an extensive knowledge of many subjects and often use word play or double entendre. Think back to Dennis Miller in his prime or almost every Coen brothers movie. *The Big Bang Theory* is highbrow humor slightly dumbed down for the masses.

> *"That field goal attempt was so far to the left it nearly decapitated Lyndon LaRouche."* —Dennis Miller

Deadpan/Dry Humor

Deadpan is more a type of delivery than a brand of humor, but it's important to mention for this reason: mastering the deadpan delivery can make even the unfunny comment seem hilarious.

Deadpan is the delivery of a joke or one-liner with zero change in emotion or body language. The tone of the joke teller is one notch above comatose. A deadpan delivery of a joke is hard to pull off, but once mastered can bring humor to even the most awkward of situations. *Curb Your Enthusiasm*, *The Office*, and the stand-up of Steven Wright highlight the brilliance of deadpan delivery.

> *"I think it's wrong that only one company makes the game Monopoly."* —Steven Wright

Puns

Henri Bergson, a famous French philosopher, defined a pun as "a sentence or utterance in which two different sets of ideas are expressed, and we are confronted with only one series of words." In non–French philosopher speak, a pun is the use of a word, or words, that have multiple meanings or sound like other words. Even unfunny people can execute a clever pun. Puns might be the hardest to write of all the different types of jokes, since puns are typically no more than a sentence or two and often require a firm grasp on language and the multiple meanings of countless words.

 Comedy Facts

Alternative comedy is a type of humor that differs from the traditional format of setup and punch line. The term was coined in the mid-1980s and can include several different types of humor including observational, satire, surrealism, slapstick, and improv. Comedian Patton Oswalt defines alternative comedy as "comedy where the audience has no pre-set expectations about the crowd, and vice versa. In comedy clubs, there tends to be a certain vibe—alternative comedy explores different types of material."

It's ironic that such a simple joke has so many different variations. There are three common types of puns:

- Homophonic puns: These are created by swapping out a word for a similar-sounding word. "Atheism is a non-prophet institution" (George Carlin).
- Homographic puns: These can be created in either one of two ways—either by inserting a word with dual meanings or substituting a word with the same spelling as the word it's replacing. "Bakers work so hard because they knead the dough." "Without geometry, life is pointless."
- Compound puns: These are strings of two or more words that sound similar to strings of different words. "My wife has a magnetic personality, because everything she picks up she charges."

The Rules of Joke-Telling

Here's a scenario you've probably seen play out millions of times, usually wherever small groups gather for an event. Whether it's a boring office function, a family gathering, a holiday party, or even a funeral, someone will seize the opportunity of having a captive audience and tell a joke.

Nine times out of ten, the joke flops—suffering a death more painful than the one experienced by the guy inside the coffin at the front of the room. And that dude died *painfully*!

 Famous Funnies

"I have six locks on my door all in a row. When I go out, I lock every other one. I figure no matter how long somebody stands there picking the locks, they are always locking three."—Elayne Boosler

It's never, *ever* the joke's fault. Every joke is funny. Human error is always to blame for a joke falling flat. Joke-telling doesn't come naturally to everyone, and even those blessed with an incredible sense of humor constantly work on joke-telling abilities.

The amazing thing about delivering jokes is that the joke teller doesn't even really have to be funny. It's all about the way the joke is told. The following five rules of joke-telling will help you be on top of your game every time you get ready to tell a joke. The moment you hear, read, or write a joke, review these five ways to make the joke your own.

Eliminate the Excess

When a joke fails, most likely it's the fault of the joke teller. One of the biggest issues many people have is the tendency to want to keep the spotlight shining on themselves for as long as possible. Because all eyes are on the person delivering the joke, the joke teller tends to elaborate on the joke's premise to prolong the attention. This craving for the spotlight leads to the addition of material that's irrelevant to the joke. Therefore, the joke fails.

 Famous Funnies

> "A lot of people are afraid of heights. Not me, I'm afraid of widths."
> —Steven Wright

If you give too much information, the listeners become uninterested. If you give way too much information, people forget they are even listening to a joke. Long-winded jokes that evolve into stories packed with unnecessary details usually end up falling flat. It's crucial to cut out as much of the fat from a joke as possible. Eliminate descriptive adjectives unless they are necessary to distinguish one character in the joke from another.

> *"A thin brunette in a tight dress and a busty blonde wearing way too much makeup walk into a department store . . ."*

Unless the size of the brunette, her attire, or the blonde's choice of makeup are pertinent to the plot or punch line of the joke, eliminate them immediately. A brunette and blonde entering a department store are the only details the crowd needs to know, and really remember, for the joke to work.

Move Slowly Forward and Never Go Backward

It's human nature to want an uncomfortable situation to end as quickly as possible while still achieving the best conceivable outcome. Telling a joke, even though it is 100 percent voluntary, is an uncomfortable situation. Ask any stand-up if he or she still gets nervous right before going onstage, no matter the level of confidence in the material, and the answer will be "Yes, of course," probably followed by a joke about the nightly jitters the stand-up faces moments before stepping in front of a microphone.

Even though people love telling jokes and getting a laugh, the uncomfortableness of joke-telling often sabotages the setup, specifics, and pending punch line. The fact that all eyes are on the jokester for the moment causes the person to rush through a setup, miss important details, and screw up the punch line. It's in these moments you'll hear joke tellers stop mid-gag to ask things like "Wait, did I say the blonde was . . ." or "Hold on, I forgot to mention . . ."

 Joke Essentials

Sometimes, the funniest joke is the one that makes fun of the teller. Self-deprecation usually gets a laugh, especially jokes that the audience knows can't possibly be true. Don't be afraid to poke fun at yourself or be the butt of the joke.

If you forget a detail that is crucial to the punch line, you're screwed, so you might as well just stop talking and fake a heart attack. Never go back and give missed details; you've already lost the audience. For the same reason, never start over. Never clutch your heart when faking a heart attack; it's too obvious. Grab for your arm.

Don't Fool with Dialogue

Some of the greatest authors in the world admit that writing believable dialogue is their Achilles' heel. If bestselling writers who spend hours a day working on their fiction can't craft believable conversations, what makes you think you can come up with dialogue for a joke off the top of your head? Keep the dialogue simple, stupid. If you find a joke that contains unnecessary dialogue, rewrite it, and then read it out loud. You'll notice the difference. Also, always make sure you're talking slowly and clearly when you're giving information, but only give stuff that's especially pertinent to the outcome. Don't add unnecessary dialogue.

If you can, keep the joke in the present tense. It gives the joke immediacy and makes it more exciting. This may seem like a minor point, but it can make all the difference. Some jokes—those involving famous people, historical events, or other entities like God or saints—may sound better in the past tense. Try the joke both ways and see which flows more easily.

Don't include any words from the punch line in the body of your joke. Not repeating the words makes the punch line more fun.

Know Your Audience

Successful football coaches usually excel in the art of locker-room speeches. This is because they not only know the Xs and Os involved in the game, but also know how to motivate a certain type of man. The typical pre-game speech involves evoking emotion, eliciting a powerful response, incorporating lots of analogies involving words like "pounding" and "grinding," and speaking in easy-to-understand terms. In other words, the coach knows his audience.

It's crucial to know your audience before you begin a joke. A group of soccer moms isn't going to appreciate your joke about the guy and the one-legged prostitute, no matter how hilarious.

 ## Ask the Comedian

Why do different people find different things funny?
This is probably a question best left for researchers, psychologists, or even psychiatrists, but we do know this much: comedy is an art, not a science. In other words, there is no exact formula that makes something funny or not funny. Much as some people appreciate a work of art while others may call it junk, jokes strike people differently. Thankfully, laughter is universal, so even if not everyone finds a particular joke funny, laughing is a shared experience.

Know the Punch Line

It shouldn't need to be said—but it needs to be said. Memorize the punch line, know it well, and even say it out loud a few times right after you've learned a new joke. You should be able to deliver it flawlessly, and with confidence, without stammering or error. If you don't know the punch line, *don't tell the joke*.

How to Write a Joke

Joke writing isn't as daunting a task as you would think. People verbally "write" jokes every day. Replay the day in your mind, remembering any of the things you might have said that elicited a laugh. It might have been a response to a coworker or an offhand comment to your wife about her sister; it's still a joke. Life is the setup, and you delivered the punch line. The setup and punch line are all you really need to construct a successful joke.

There are four key steps to joke writing:

1. Find the humor in a topic
2. Find the common ground
3. Find a twist
4. Perfect the punch line and build out

Find the Humor in a Topic

The topic can be anything from the recognizable to the obscure, but the key is to find humor in the parts of life you know the best. A popular expression in all forms of writing is to "write about what you know," and the same goes for joke writing—joke about what you know.

If you're a delivery man, write jokes about your job. If you spend weekends pounding out miles for exercise, find the humor in the activity of running. Do you wake up and eat the same breakfast every morning? There is probably a hilarious joke waiting to be written about that.

Find the Common Ground

Now that you've chosen your topic, find the common ground that connects you with an audience or the shared experience that will eventually elicit a laugh.

Think again about running for exercise. According to a report from *Running USA* published in 2012, there were around 25,000 marathon finishers in the United States in 1976. In 2011, the number was roughly 518,000. That's more than half a million people who understand the culture of running and would probably laugh at a joke about their passion.

Now, imagine all the people who run for exercise, but would never dream of attempting a marathon. The number is probably much higher than those who do run marathons. If you add in all the people who hate running and exercise and just want to laugh at people who like the sport, well, you've got almost the entire world.

You've identified the common ground with your audience, and you've also found the setup.

 ## Joke Essentials

It is believed that 80 percent of people learn through visuals. If this is true, then joke tellers should try and be more animated when telling jokes. Don't be afraid to act out a joke or even use impromptu props or even other people during the storytelling aspect of a joke.

Find a Twist

Why do people love magicians? It's not their cool outfits or suitcases full of rabbits and handkerchiefs; it's the element of surprise that comes with even the simplest magic trick. Imagine that a joke is like a magic trick. People don't want to see the punch line coming. This is what's known as the "twist" or surprise of a joke.

Again, you can return to the common ground of running and exercise. Here is an example.

"I took up running last year. I hired a trainer. He called me on the morning of my first run and told me to 'wear loose clothing.' I told him if I had loose clothing I sure as hell wouldn't bother running."

If you break the joke down, you'll see the topic is still running and exercise. The common ground is the relatable idea of hiring another person to force us into exercise. The twist is that the joke is not specifically about running, but about the absurdity of why people exercise.

Perfect the Punch Line and Build Out

The punch line is always a work in progress. Even if it gets a laugh, it can always be tweaked and perfected. Now that you've written one joke about a topic, write jokes building on the topic or even building on the premise of the loose-fitting clothing. There are countless ways to expand on one simple premise.

The most important part is that you've written a joke.

CHAPTER 2

Families and Relationship Jokes

Everyone's family is unique unto itself. Brothers, sisters, mothers, fathers, cousins, and so on. They are the people you grow up with, grow to love (sometimes hate), and eventually grow old with. Hopefully, they come to your funeral. If they don't, don't you dare go to their funeral! It's easiest to joke about the people you know the best. Enjoy these jokes about your own flesh and blood.

Families

✴ TWO SISTERS, A BLONDE AND a brunette, inherit the family ranch. Unfortunately, after just a few years of trying to run the operation, they are in financial trouble. In order to keep the bank from repossessing the property, they need to purchase an expensive bull so they can breed their own stock. The brunette looks over their finances and decides to take their last $600 out west to another ranch, where a man has a prize bull for sale. Before leaving, she tells her blonde sister, "If I decide to buy the bull, I'll contact you to drive out west and haul it home."

The brunette arrives at the man's ranch, inspects the bull, and decides she does want to buy it. The man tells her that he can sell it for $599 and no less. She agrees, pays the man all she has except for one dollar, and asks for a lift to the nearest town to send her sister a telegram. She walks into the telegraph office and says, "I want to send a telegram to my sister telling her that I've bought a bull for our ranch. I need her to hitch the trailer to our pickup truck and drive out here so we can haul it home." The telegraph operator explains that he'll be glad to help her, then adds, "But it's going to cost you 99 cents per word." With only one dollar left, the brunette realizes that she'll only be able to send her sister one single word. After thinking for a few minutes, she says, "I want you to send her the word 'comfortable.'" The telegraph operator shakes his head. "How is she ever going to know that you want her to hitch a trailer to your pickup truck and drive out here to haul that bull back to your ranch if you just write the word 'comfortable'?" The brunette sister explains, "My sister is a blonde and a very slow reader. Com-for-ta-ble."

 ## Joke Essentials

Don't steal jokes from stand-up comics, especially popular stand-up comics. Jokes are material. If you're telling a joke, you don't have to credit a comic exactly—no one is going to come looking for you—but after the joke say, "I heard that on the radio the other day" or "I saw a guy tell that joke live a few years back." If it's an older joke, with an unknown origin, there is really nothing you can do about crediting the source. An audience will be able to tell new material from an old standard.

✱ A HUSBAND AND WIFE ARE visited by the wife's family during the holidays. Her mother is a stickler for her food intake, and will only eat organic and fresh foods. The husband goes to the store with specific instructions on the type of foods to buy. "Excuse me," the man asks the grocer, "are these vegetables sprayed with any harmful chemicals or pesticides that could kill a person?" "Nope," answers the grocer proudly. "Okay," says the man, "I guess I'll just have to do that part myself."

✷ A YOUNG MAN HAS FINALLY saved up enough money to buy his own house. It is just a few houses down from the house he grew up in, the home his parents still live in. On the day he moves in, he invites some friends over, turns on some music, and sits on the porch while they all drink beers. "The best part is I don't have to listen to my parents anymore." A phone call interrupts his speech. He retreats into the house and after a few minutes comes back out after turning down the music. "Who was on the phone?" a friend asks. "Oh, it was my dad," the man says. "He was calling to tell me to turn down the music. There are people trying to sleep."

 Comedy Facts

At the end of World War II, returning members of the armed forces craved stand-up comedy because of wartime concerts put on by famous acts visiting troops. The rise of the postwar comedians also coincided with the rise of television and radio.

✷ I ALWAYS CARRY A PICTURE of my wife and kids in my wallet. I do it to remind me why there is no money in there.

Parenting

✷ PARENTS SPEND THE FIRST TWELVE months of their kid's life teaching him to walk and talk and then spend the next twenty years telling him to sit down and shut up.

✷ A MAN PULLS OVER TO the side of the road after a police cruiser flashes him to do so. "How long have you been riding around without a taillight?" asks the officer. "Oh, no!" screams the man, jumping out of the car. "Wait 'til my family finds out!" "Where's your family?" the officer asks. "They're in the trailer that was hitched to the car!"

✱ A YOUNG BOY RUNS INTO the street to get his baseball without looking both ways. He is hit by an oncoming car and breaks both of his legs. After his legs are in casts and he is sent home, his mother asks him if he's learned his lesson. "Are you going to run out into the street anymore?" she asks. "No way," he says, tugging at his casts. "Next time I'm sending my sister."

✱ TWO HOUSEWIVES ARE HAVING COFFEE while their children play in the living room. The first woman is very well off, while the second scrapes by on just her husband's salary. The first woman is bragging about her new appliances and says, "We've even got a new toaster that can send a message to the television that the toast is done." "That's nothing," replies the second woman, "our toaster lets us know the toast is done by setting off the fire alarm."

 Famous Funnies

> "I was the kid next door's imaginary friend."—Emo Philips

✱ A MAN IN THE GROCERY store notices a woman with a three-year-old girl in her cart. As they pass the cookie section, the little girl screams for cookies. The mother says, "Now Missy, we only have a few more aisles to go—don't throw a fit. It won't be long." In the candy aisle, the little girl whines for candy. The mother says, "There, there, Missy, don't cry. Two more aisles, and we'll be checking out." When they get to the checkout stand, the little girl howls for gum. The mother says, reassuringly, "Missy, we'll be done in five minutes, and then you can go home and have a bottle and a nice snooze." In the parking lot, the man stops the woman to compliment her. "I couldn't help noticing how patient you were with little Missy," he says. The mother sighs, "Oh, no—my little girl's name is Francine. I'm Missy."

✳ A WOMAN GIVES BIRTH AT a hospital and the doctor asks, "What will you name her?" The woman thinks and says, "I think I'll name her Sarah!" The doctor says, "I'm sorry to inform you miss, but Sarah is not available. But you can try Sarah_2045 or 99_Sarah!"

✳ THE ODD THING ABOUT PARENTING is that by the time you are experienced at your job, you are unemployed.

✳ A MOTHER IS DRIVING HER little girl to her friend's house for a play date. "Mommy," the little girl asks, "how old are you?"

"Honey, you are not supposed to ask a lady her age," the mother replies. "It's not polite."

"Okay," the little girl says. "How much do you weigh?"

"Now really," the mother says, "those are personal questions and are really none of your business."

Undaunted, the little girl asks, "Why did you and Daddy get a divorce?"

"That's enough questions, young lady! Honestly!" The exasperated mother walks away as the two friends begin to play.

"My mom won't tell me anything about her," the little girl says to her friend.

"Well," says the friend, "all you need to do is look at her driver's license. It has everything on it."

Later that night the little girl says to her mother, "I know how old you are. You are thirty-two."

The mother is surprised and asks, "How did you find that out?"

"I also know that you weigh 130 pounds."

The mother is past surprised and shocked now. "How in heaven's name did you find that out?"

"And," the little girl says triumphantly, "I know why you and Daddy got a divorce."

"Oh really?" the mother asks. "Why?"

"Because you got an F in sex."

✱ POLITICIANS AND DIAPERS HAVE ONE thing in common: They should both be changed regularly and for exactly the same reason.

✱ A MOTHER TRAVELED ACROSS THE country to watch her only son get married and graduate from the Air Force on the exact same day. "Thank you for coming," the son said. "It means so much." "Of course I'd be here," the mother replied. "It's not every day a mom watches her son get his wings and have them clipped all in one day."

 ## Comedy Facts

Character comedy derives humor from an invented persona. The persona is often a part of the personality of the creator, just played to a grander scale for the amusement of the audience. Popular character comedies include Paul Reubens as man-child Pee-wee Herman; Rowan Atkinson as Mr. Bean; Sacha Baron Cohen as Ali G, Borat, or Brüno; and Steve Coogan as Alan Partridge.

✱ IF YOU WANT A LARGE family, the best plan is to have as many kids at one time as possible. Then they'll put you on TV and you'll get a ton of free stuff from other Americans.

✱ "DENISE, WHY DID YOU JUST kick your brother in the stomach?" exclaimed the angry mother. "It was an accident, Mom! He turned around!"

✱ A FAMILY TAKES A TRIP to Disney World. After seven exhausting days, they head home. As they drive away, the son waves out the window and says, "Goodbye, Mickey." The daughter waves and says, "Goodbye, Minnie." Dad waves and cries, "Goodbye, money."

✱ JOHNNY IS WORKING HARD AT his mother's desk, scribbling on a piece of paper. His mother asks, "Are you writing a letter to your little girlfriend, son?"

"Nope," he answers. "I'm writing a letter to mail to myself."

"Oh." She smiles. "What is the letter going to say?"

"How should I know?" he responds. "I haven't gotten it in the mail yet."

 Famous Funnies

"An optimist sees a zombie as half alive. A pessimist sees a zombie and says, 'Yep, I knew this would happen.'"—Tim Siedell

✷ A MOTHER CALLS HER DAUGHTER on the phone to tell her she's got diabetes. "Now, I don't want you to think I've got diabetes because I'm overweight," the mother stresses. "It's because it runs in the family."

"I think you're wrong," the girl tells her mother. "It's because no one runs in our family."

✷ SARAH WATCHES AS HER MOTHER tries on an expensive fur coat in a high-end department store. "Do you realize," Sarah says, "that some poor, dumb animal had to suffer just for you to wear that coat?" Sarah's mother turns to her and snaps, "Think about how much I've suffered! And don't call your father an animal."

✷ PASSING THROUGH HIS SON'S COLLEGE town late one night, a father decides to drop in and pay his kid a visit. The father knocks on the fraternity house door. No one answers. He knocks louder, but still no answer. He begins to bang angrily on the door. Finally, a head pops out of a window on the second floor. "You need something, pal?" a frat brother asks from the window.

"Yes, does Billy Powers live here?" the father asks.

"Yeah," says the frat brother, "just dump him on the steps and we'll grab him in the morning."

✷ "HOW'S YOUR BIG PSYCHOLOGY TERM paper coming?" a mother asks her son at breakfast while he is visiting for fall break.

"It's going well," he says. "My professor suggested I check out some resources online." "And you've found a lot of help on the Internet?" the mother asks. "Totally," the student replies. "I've found more than a few websites where I can get a paper written for pretty cheap."

✱ TWO FRUSTRATED STAY-AT-HOME DADS ARE talking on the playground. "I tried to discipline the kid last night by sending him to his room but there are more toys, gadgets, and games in his room than in a big-box store. I'm not sure what to do anymore."

"Do what I do," says the second dad. "I send my kid to my room. There is nothing in there."

✱ A THREE-YEAR-OLD WALKS OVER TO a pregnant lady while waiting with his mother in a doctor's waiting room. "Why is your stomach so big?" he asks.

"I'm having a baby," she replies.

"Is the baby in your stomach?" he asks, wide-eyed.

"Yes, it is," she says.

"Is it a good baby?" he asks with a puzzled look.

"Oh, yes. A really good baby," the lady replies.

Shocked and surprised, he asks: "Then why did you eat him?"

✱ A MAN BUYS A LIE-DETECTING robot that slaps people who lie, and decides to test it out at dinner. He asks his son, "Did you go to school today?" The son replies "Yes," and the robot slaps him. The sons says, "All right, I went to the movies."

The father asks, "What did you see?" and the son replies, "*Toy Story 3*." The robot slaps him again, and the son says, "Okay, okay! It was an adult film."

His father snorts and says, "When I was your age we didn't know what pornography was!" This time the robot slaps the father.

The mother sips her coffee and retorts, "Ha! He's your son, after all," and the robot slaps her.

✳ TWO MEN ARE TALKING OVER drinks when the first man admits to the second, "You're not going to believe this, but I once went twelve years without alcohol, drugs, and sex." "Wow, that is surprising," the second man admits.

"Yeah," the first man adds, "but holy cow did my old man know how to throw a thirteenth-birthday bash!"

✳ ONE DAY A MOM WAS out and dad was in charge of their just-turned-three son, Ben. Someone had given Ben a little tea set as a birthday gift, and it was one of his favorite toys. Daddy was in the living room engrossed in the evening news when Ben brought Daddy a little cup of "tea," which was just water. After several cups of "tea" and lots of praise for such yummy tea from Daddy, Mom came home. Dad made her wait in the living room to watch Ben bring him a cup of tea, because it was "just the cutest thing!" Mom waited, and sure enough, the kid came down the hall with a cup of tea for Daddy. She watched him drink it up and then said to him, "Did it ever occur to you that the only place Ben can reach to get water is the toilet?"

✳ A MAN IS DROWNING HIS sorrows at his local bar. The bartender, recognizing him as a regular, asks him why he is so down. "I just got back from parent-teacher conferences at my kid's school. His teacher told me and his mom he's the worst student in the class and will probably have to repeat the fourth grade."

"Man, that's awful," the bartender replies. "I feel really bad about that."

"Thanks," the father replies, "but you'll probably feel even worse after I tell you he's thirteen."

✳ A DAD WAS TRYING TO teach his kid about the evils of drinking. He put one worm in a glass of water and another worm in a glass of whiskey. The worm in the water survived, but the worm in the whiskey curled up and died almost immediately. "All right, kid," the father began, "what does this little experiment prove to you about drinking?"

"Well," the kid replied thoughtfully, "it proves that if a person drinks alcohol he probably won't get worms."

✳ A GUY CALLS 911 IN a panic. "My wife is having a baby! Her contractions are only one minute apart!"

"Calm down," the 911 operator says. "Is this her first child?"

"No, you idiot!" the guy shouts. "This is her husband!"

 ## Ask the Comedian

What is a comedy roast?
A roast is an event in which an individual is "honored" by friends and acquaintances. The individual being roasted is usually subjected to comedic insults, outlandish true and untrue stories, and heartwarming tributes. The implication is that the roastee is able to take the jokes as a sign of adoration. At the end, the roastee is usually given the opportunity to turn the tables on the people roasting him or her. It's considered an honor in the comedy community to be roasted.

✳ A RICH MAN IS TRYING to find a birthday gift for his daughter when he sees a poor man with a beautiful white horse. He tells the man that he will give him $500 for the horse. The poor man replies, "I don't know, mister, it don't look so good," and walks away. The next day the rich man comes back and offers the poor man $1,000 for the horse. The poor man says, "I don't know, mister, it don't look so good." On the third day the rich man offers the poor man $2,000 for the horse, and says he won't take "no" for an answer. The poor man agrees, and the rich man takes the horse home. The rich man's daughter loves her present. She climbs onto the horse, then gallops right into a tree. The rich man rushes back over to the poor man's house, demanding an explanation for the horse's blindness. The poor man replied, "I told you it don't look so good!"

✳ LITTLE DARREN RUNS INTO HIS house and asks his mom, "Can little girls have babies?"

"No, of course not!" replies his mom. Darren runs back outside and yells to his friends, "It's cool, we can play that game again!"

✳ A LITTLE GIRL ASKS HER mother, "How did the human race appear?" The mother answers, "Well, God made Adam and Eve and then they had kids. So all mankind was made." Two days later the little girl asks her father the exact same question. The father answers, "Many years ago, there were monkeys from which the entire human race evolved." The confused little girl returns to her mother and says, "Mom, you told me the human race was created by God and Dad said man developed from monkeys. Why do you have different stories?" The mother answers, "Well, I was referring to my side of the family and your dad was talking about his side."

✳ IF YOU WANT TO PREPARE your kid for the future, don't teach him to subtract—teach him to deduct!

✳ BEING A PARENT IS VERY similar to serving time behind bars in jail, except in this case, the jail follows you around and wants to talk about Teenage Mutant Ninja Turtles all day.

✳ A LITTLE LEAGUE COACH GATHERS his team in the dugout before the big championship game. "Whatever happens today," he begins, "I want to see good sportsmanship, no outbursts or tantrums, no yelling at the umps, and absolutely no sore losers. Does everyone understand?" The team members all nod in agreement. "Good," the coach says, "now I want you all to go out there and repeat that to your fathers."

Children

✳ IT IS THE FIRST DAY of kindergarten and the teacher is going around the room asking everyone what their father does for work.

The first child raises her hand and says, "My dad is a policeman. He sends bad guys to jail!"

The second child raises his hand and says, "My dad is a fireman. He puts out fires!"

The third child slowly puts up his hand and tells the class, "My dad died of a heart attack." Trying to end the uncomfortable silence in the room, the teacher asks the student, "What did your dad do before he died?"

"Well," the boy replies, "he went 'UGGGGHHHHHH, I think I'm dying.'"

✱ ON THE FIRST DAY OF school, a first-grader hands a note from his mother to the teacher. The note reads, "The opinions expressed by this child are not necessarily those of his parents."

✱ A SMALL BOY SWALLOWS SOME coins and is taken to a hospital. When his grandmother telephones to ask how he is, the nurse tells her, "No change yet."

✱ THE THREE WISE MEN VISIT Joseph and Mary in the stable to see the newborn son. The extremely tall wise man hits his head on the door frame and exclaims, "Jesus Christ!" Joseph looks at Mary and says, "Write that down—that's much better than Clyde."

✱ A STUDENT WALKS INTO HIS homeroom and asks his teacher, "Would I get in trouble for something I didn't do?" The teacher answers, "No, of course not." The student sits in his seat and says, "Good. Well, in that case, I might as well tell you now I didn't do my term paper."

✱ A TEACHER WANTS HER CLASS to learn about self-esteem, so she invites students who think they are stupid to stand up. One kid stands up, and the teacher is surprised—he is a bright student, after all. She asks him, "Why did you stand up?"

He answers, "I didn't want to leave you standing up by yourself."

✳ TWO BOYS ARE ARGUING WHEN the teacher enters the class-room. The teacher says, "What are you two arguing about?"

One boy answers, "We found a ten-dollar bill and decided who-ever tells the biggest lie gets to keep it."

"You two should be ashamed of yourselves," says the teacher. "When I was your age, I didn't even know what a lie was." The boys look at each other and hand the ten dollars to the teacher.

 Famous Funnies

"A two-year-old is kind of like having a blender, but you don't have a top for it."—Jerry Seinfeld

✳ A WOMAN HAS TWINS, AND gives them up for adoption. One of them goes to a family in Egypt and is named "Amal." The other goes to a fam-ily in Spain; they name him "Juan." Years later, Juan sends a picture of himself to his birth mom. Upon receiving the picture, she tells her husband that she wished she also had a picture of Amal. Her husband responds, "But they are twins. If you've seen Juan, you've seen Amal."

✳ A YOUNG BOY RUNS INTO the house and excitedly shows his mother a fifty-dollar bill he found in the park. "Are you sure it was lost?" the mother asks.

"I'm positive," the boy replies. "I even saw the guy looking for it."

✳ A BOY IS FALLING ASLEEP at the dinner table after a day at school plus two hours of track practice and a guitar lesson. "I'm too tired to do my homework," he tells his mother at the table. "Can't you just do it for me?"

The mother responds, "I can't do that, honey. It wouldn't be right."

The tired boy responds, "That doesn't matter, as long as I hand something in."

✳ A TEACHER CALLS ON JASON during a spelling lesson.

"Jason, how do you spell 'establishment'?" Jason answers, "E-S-T-A-B-L-U-S-H-M-E-N-D-T."

"I'm sorry, Jason, that's not right."

"I'm sure it's not right," Jason responds, "but you asked how I spell it."

✳ A LITTLE BOY IS TAKING his time walking to school. One of his classmates, running past him because he's also late, yells back to the boy, "You better run! You're going to be late!" The little boy yells ahead to his friend, "I've got time. School's open until 3:30."

✳ A FATHER COMES HOME FROM the grocery store with an immense bag of candy. He says to his four kids, "I'm going to give this entire bag of candy to the person who never talks back to Mommy and always does exactly what she asks. Now who do we think is going to get them?"

The oldest child replies, "Well obviously, you are."

✳ A TEACHER ASKS HER CLASS, "True or False? The Declaration of Independence was written in Philadelphia."

"False," says a boy in the back. "It was written in ink."

✳ A SCHOOL TEACHER NOTICES A student is getting much better with numbers than he was just a few weeks earlier. "Your counting has improved," the teacher tells him after class.

"Thanks," the boy says. "My dad will be glad to hear that. He's been working on them with me every night and weekend."

"Fantastic," the teacher replies. "So here's a quick quiz—what comes after nine?"

"Ten," the boy replies enthusiastically.

"Right, and what comes after ten?" the teacher quizzes.

"The jack!" the boy answers.

✳ A TEACHER WALKS OVER TO the desk of a student during an exam and says to him, "I hope I didn't just see you looking over at your neighbor's answers."

The boy replies, "Yeah, I hope you didn't see it either."

* A TEACHER WAS GIVING A history lesson when she called Tim up to the front of the class. "Tim," she said, "point to America on the map." Tim pointed to the United States. "Very good," the teacher said. "Now can anyone tell me who discovered America?" Samantha raised her hand and said, "Tim just did. Now who's the one not paying attention in class?"

* A SECOND-GRADE TEACHER IS GIVING her daily grammar lesson. "Tammy," the teacher calls out to a girl in the first row of class, "please use 'I' in a sentence."

"I is," Tammy begins, but is immediately interrupted.

"No, Tammy," the teacher says, "that's incorrect. You always say 'I am.'"

"All right," Tammy says. "I am the letter that comes after H."

* "I DON'T WANT THIS TO sound like a threat," the young boy tells his teacher, "but last night my dad said if my grades don't start improving, someone was getting a butt-kicking."

* "WHAT DID YOU LEARN IN school today?" a mother asks her seven-year-old daughter while making her a snack after school.

"Today the teacher showed us how to make babies."

The mother drops the plate of cookies onto the counter. Afraid to hear the answer, she finally asks, "How?"

Her daughter replies, "Well first, you drop the 'y,' and then . . ."

* A TEACHER TELLS HER CLASS that the highest score on the Spanish exam was earned by Alison. "You see, class, this is what happens when your parents take an interest in your schoolwork and speak the language at home to help you learn."

"If that's the case," says Billy, "I'm going to kill it on my geometry test. My parents are total squares who constantly talk in circles."

✱ A SUNDAY SCHOOL TEACHER ASKS her students about the path to heaven. "If I sell all of my possessions and give the money to the needy, will I go to heaven?"

"No," replies the class.

"If I quit my job and spent my days helping the homeless and the orphans, will I go to heaven?" she asks.

"No," they answer again.

"Okay," she asks in frustration, "then just how will I get to heaven?"

A little boy in the back raises his hand and answers, "The first thing you have to do to get to heaven is die."

✱ DURING A DINNER PARTY, THE hosts' two little children enter the dining room totally nude and walk slowly around the table. The parents are so embarrassed that they pretend nothing is happening and keep the conversation going. The guests cooperate and also continue as if nothing extraordinary is happening. After going all the way around the room the children leave, and there is a moment of silence at the table, during which one of the children is heard saying, "You see, it is vanishing cream!"

✱ A CHURCH PASTOR IS INVITED to dinner at the house of a parishioner. The pastor sits at the table with the family. The mom requests her daughter, age six, say grace before the meal. She sits in silence. "It's okay, dear," the mother calms her. "You can do it. Just repeat what you heard Daddy say before breakfast this morning."

The little girl folds her hands, bows her head, and says in a loud voice, "Oh Christ, why did you invite the pastor over for dinner tonight?"

✱ A KID COMES HOME FROM school and asks, "Dad, can you write in the dark?"

The dad thinks about it for a moment and answers, "I think so. What is it you want me to write?"

His son hands him a piece of paper and says, "Your name on this report card."

* TED HAS JUST LEARNED HIS ABCs and is scared to death to recite them in front of the class. The teacher, though, tells him that the best way to conquer his fears would be to just go up in front of the class and do it, best he can. Trembling, Ted stands in front of the class and begins: "ABCDEFGHIJKLMNOQRSTUVWXYZ."

"Very good, Ted," the teacher says from the back of the room, "but you forgot the P. Where's the P?"

Ted replies, "It's running down my leg."

* A TEACHER KEEPS A STUDENT after class to discuss a recent essay he handed in for homework. "This essay is identical to the essay your brother handed in last year," the teacher tells the student.

"Well of course it is," the student replies. "We share the dog."

* A KID IS LATE FOR school one day. "I had to take the bull down to mate with the heifer," he explains to the teacher.

"Well couldn't your father have done that?" the teacher asks after class.

"Sure," the boy replies. "But the bull would have done a better job."

* A LITTLE BOY AND LITTLE girl are getting clean in a bathtub. Suddenly the little girl looks down at the boy and asks, "Can I touch it?"

"No way," he answers, looking down and then back at her. "You already broke yours off!"

* THE SECRETARY IN THE HIGH school attendance office answers her phone just before school starts for the day. "I'm calling to let you know that Tom Gillespie won't be in school today. He's not feeling good."

"Okay," the secretary says suspiciously, "and who is this speaking?"

"It's my father," the voice replies.

* A WOMAN IS TRYING HARD to get the ketchup out of the glass bottle onto her daughter's lunch. During her struggle, the phone rings, so

she asks the four-year-old girl to answer the phone. After a moment, the girl says to the person on the other line, "My mommy can't come to the phone to talk to you right now. She's hitting the bottle again."

✱ A FATHER CONFRONTS HIS YOUNG son in the backyard. "I heard you skipped school today to go to the beach with your friends."

"That's a lie!" the boy shouts. "And I've got the movie stub to prove it."

✱ A SECOND-GRADE TEACHER TELLS HER class one morning, "We're going to do vocabulary lessons today. Who can use the word 'definitely' in a sentence?"

Mary raises her hand and exclaims, "I can!"

The teacher says, "Go ahead, Mary. What's the sentence?"

The little girl replies, "The sky is definitely blue."

"That's good, Mary," says the teacher. "But the sky can also be gray or white."

Sam raises his hand and states, "Grass is definitely green."

The teacher says, "That's a good try, Sam, but grass can also be brown."

Johnny raises his hand and asks the teacher, "Do farts have lumps in them?"

The teacher says, "Johnny, that has nothing to do with the lesson, and is also a terrible thing to ask. No, farts do not have lumps. What would possess you to ask such a question?"

Johnny replies, "I wanted to make sure I am correct in saying I definitely just crapped in my pants."

✱ A STRANGER AT THE PARK is watching a young boy play in front of his young mother. After a few minutes of the boy clucking incessantly, the man asks, "Why does your son repeatedly say 'cluck, cluck, cluck'?"

The young mother replies, "Because he thinks he's a chicken."

"Why don't you tell him he's not a chicken?" the stranger asks.

"Well," says the mom, "because we really need the eggs."

✳ A LITTLE KID GETS ON a city bus, sits right behind the driver, and starts talking loudly. "If my dad was a bull and my mom was a cow, I'd be a little bull." The driver gets annoyed as the kid continues to talk in his ear. "If my dad was a rooster and my mom was a hen, I would be a little chick."

The kid goes on and on using all the animals he knows, until finally the bus driver turns and yells in the boy's face, "Well, what if your dad was a bum and your mom was a drunk?"

The kid smiles and replies, "Well, then I'd probably be a bus driver."

✳ CHILDREN LEFT ALONE IN THE back seat can cause accidents, which is ironic considering that accidents in the back seat can cause children.

✳ A LITTLE GIRL AND HER mom are in church. In the middle of the sermon, the little girl tells her mother she's going to be sick. Her mother tells her to go outside and throw up in the bushes behind the church. The little girl leaves and comes back after about five minutes. Her mother asks her if she threw up. "Yes," the girl says. "But I didn't have to go all the way outside. There was a box near the front door that said 'For the Sick.'"

✳ FOUR EXPECTANT FATHERS PACE BACK and forth in a hospital waiting room while their wives are in labor. The nurse enters and tells the first man, "Congratulations, you're the father of twins!"

"What a coincidence," the man says. "I work for the Minnesota Twins baseball team."

A little later, the nurse returns and tells the second man, "You are the father of triplets!"

"That's really an incredible coincidence," he answers, "considering I work for the 3M Corporation."

An hour later, the nurse tells the third man that his wife has just given birth to quadruplets. The man says, "That's insane! I work for the Four Seasons. What a weird coincidence!"

After hearing this latest news, everyone's attention turns to the fourth expectant father, who has just fainted. He slowly regains consciousness and whispers to the attending nurse, "I knew I shouldn't have taken that job at Books-A-Million."

✸ A MOTHER DECIDES TO TAKE an overnight flight to visit her husband at his latest military assignment. She wearily arrives at the base with all nine of their children so she can take them along to see their father. Collecting their suitcases, the family of ten enters the cramped customs area. A young customs official watches the entourage in disbelief. "Ma'am," he says to the mother, "do all these children and this luggage belong to you?"

"Yes, sir," the exhausted mother replies, "they're all mine."

The customs agent begins his interrogation. "Ma'am, do you have any weapons, contraband, or illegal drugs in your possession?"

"Sir," she calmly answers, "if I'd had any of those items, I would have used them by now."

 Famous Funnies

"Having children is like living in a frat house: nobody sleeps, everything's broken, and there's a lot of throwing up."—Ray Romano

✸ A YOUNG BOY IS SCARED of monsters living under his bed. To make him feel safer at night, his parents fill an empty spray bottle with water and label it "Monster Repellent."

"If you think a monster is coming out from under your bed," the dad explains, "just spray this at him. This will keep you safe from any and all monsters."

The young boy is skeptical, but keeps it at his bedside. At breakfast the next morning his father asks, "Were you safe last night?" The boy nods yes. "Good," the dad replies, "but you know, son, there really aren't any monsters under your bed. Monsters don't exist."

The boy looks at his father and asks, "If monsters don't exist, then why do they make Monster Repellent?"

✳ A MOTHER DROPS HER YOUNG son at a friend's house for a play date. An hour later, she gets a call from the play date's mom. "I just caught your son trying to play doctor with my daughter."

The first mom laughs and says, "Well, I think it's only natural that young kids have an interest in sex."

"Sex?" the second mother asks. "What does sex have to do with your son trying to remove my daughter's appendix?"

✳ A YOUNG BOY IS LISTENING to the radio in the car with his father. "Dad, what music did you like growing up?"

"I was a huge fan of Led Zeppelin," the father replies.

"Who?" the son asks.

"Yeah," the dad responds, "I liked them too."

✳ A MOTHER IS EXPLAINING FIRE safety to her young kids. They go over fire evacuation, how to get to safety, and where to meet in the yard to make sure everyone is safe. "For example," the mother asks, "let's say this afternoon I accidentally start a fire while making your lunch. What would you do?"

The oldest child replies, "We'd all meet in the yard and make you take us to McDonald's for lunch."

✳ TWO YOUNG BOYS ARE AT the wedding of their uncle. It is his third marriage in ten years. "How many times is a person allowed to get married?" the first boy asks.

"I think something like sixteen," says the other boy.

"How did you get that number?" the first boy asks.

"Well," he responds, "the preacher said it in the ceremony: 'Four better, four worse, four richer, and four poorer.'"

✳ A BOSS WONDERS WHY ONE of his most valued employees has phoned in sick one day. Needing the employee to solve an urgent problem with one of the main computers, the boss dials the employee's home phone number. He is greeted by a child's whisper.

"Hello?"

"Is your daddy home?" he asks.

"Yes," whispers the young voice.

"May I talk with him?"

The child whispers, "No."

Surprised and wanting to talk with an adult, the boss asks, "Is your mommy there?"

"Yes," the boy responds.

"May I talk with her?"

Again the young voice whispers, "No."

Hoping there is somebody with whom he could leave a message, the boss asks, "Is anybody else there?"

"Yes," whispers the child, "a policeman."

Wondering what a cop would be doing at his employee's home, the boss asks, "May I speak with the policeman?"

"No, he's busy," whispers the child.

"Busy doing what?"

"Talking to Mommy and Daddy and the fireman," the boy whispers.

Growing more worried as he hears what sounds like a helicopter through the telephone, the boss asks, "What is that noise?"

"A hello-copper," answers the whispering voice.

"What is going on there?" demands the boss.

Again, whispering, the child answers, "The search team just landed the hello-copper." Alarmed and concerned, the boss asks, "What are they searching for?"

Still whispering, the young voice replies with a muffled giggle, "Me!"

✳ TWO YOUNG BOYS, BOBBY AND Tommy, are sharing a hospital room. After getting to know each other a little bit, Bobby eventually asks Tommy, "Hey, what're you in the hospital for anyway?"

"I'm getting my tonsils out," explains Tommy. "And I'm a little worried."

"Oh, don't worry about it," Bobby says. "I had my tonsils out and it was actually not so bad. I got to eat all the ice cream and Jell-O I wanted for two weeks!"

"Oh yeah?" replies Tommy. "That's not bad. So, Bobby, how about you? What are you here for?"

"I'm getting a circumcision, whatever that is," Bobby answers.

"Oh my god! A circumcision?" Tommy cries. "I got one of those when I was a baby. I couldn't walk for two years!"

✳ A TEACHER ASKS HER CLASS their favorite afterschool snacks. "Decklyn," the teacher calls to the new student in the back of the room, "what's your favorite afterschool snack?"

"Nuts," he replies.

"Very good," the teacher replies. "What kind of nuts? Peanuts? Pine nuts?"

The boy shakes his head and answers, "Doughnuts."

✳ A CENSUS TAKER KNOCKS ON the front door of a young woman home alone with her four kids. After introducing himself, the census taker asks, "How many children do you have?"

"Four," the frazzled mom answers. The census taker jots down the answer and asks as a follow-up, "Can I have their names, please?"

The woman replies, "Well there is Eenie, Meenie, Mienie, and the youngest is George." The census taker chuckles a little and replies, "Why did you end up naming your fourth child 'George'?"

"Because by that point," the mother answers, "we were more than positive we didn't want any Moe."

* A WIFE PHONES HER HUSBAND at work to tell him she's taking the kids out for the day. "One of them wants to go the zoo and the other wants to go to the movies. Then they said we should do both."

"No way," the father says, "that's too expensive. It's either one or the other. Which do you prefer?"

The mother responds, "I prefer the older one."

* THREE YOUNG BOYS ARE FIGHTING over whose dad is the better man.

"My dad is so good he can shoot an arrow, run after it, get in front of it, and catch it in his bare hands."

"That's nothing!" exclaims the second boy. "My dad is so good that he can shoot a gun, run after the bullet, jump in front of it, and catch it in his teeth!"

The third boy laughs. "I've got you both beat," he tells his friends. "My dad's better because he works for the government. He's so fast that he gets off work at five o'clock and is somehow home by four-thirty every day."

* A LIFEGUARD ASKS A MOTHER to scold her son for urinating in the public pool. "It's perfectly natural," the mother says, "for young children to urinate in the pool. Plenty of children at this pool do it. I don't see why my son doing it is such a big deal."

The lifeguard pulls down his sunglasses and replies, "Well, all the other kids aren't doing it off the diving board."

Teens and Tweens

* A TEENAGER IS TALKING TO her friend before class. "For the prom, I'm renting a limo, spending $500 on a new dress, and bringing in the best makeup artist in the state to do my hair."

A teacher overhears the conversation and remarks, "Wow, that's more than I spent for my wedding!"

The girl replies, "Yeah, well you can get married three or four times, but you only go to prom once."

✳ WHAT'S THE ONE THING THAT keeps most teen men out of college? High school.

✳ ON HIS EIGHTEENTH BIRTHDAY, A son announces to his parents that he is no longer abiding by their curfew. "I'm an adult now," he says, "and you can't stop me from exiting and entering the house any time I want."

"You're half right," says his dad. "We can't stop you from leaving the house, but we can stop you from coming back in."

✳ A YOUNG GIRL IS LEARNING to drive with her father when suddenly the brakes stop working. "I can't stop the car!" she cries out to her father.

"Okay, calm down," the father replies. "Just take your foot off the pedal, wait for the car to slow down, and then aim for something that looks cheap."

✳ "HOW DARE YOU DISOBEY YOUR mother!" a father yells at his daughter. "Do you think you're better than I am or something?"

✳ JOSH AND HIS MOM GO to an all-you-can-eat restaurant. Josh returns to the table, his plate full, for the fifth time. "Josh!" exclaims his mother. "Doesn't it embarrass you that people have seen you go up to the buffet five times?"

"Not at all," says Josh, "I just tell them I'm filling up the plate for you!"

✳ "HOW DID THE CAR END up in the living room?" a furious father asks his son.

"Simple," the boy replies. "I made a right at the kitchen."

✳ THERE'S FIFTEEN MINUTES LEFT BEFORE curfew in a small town. A man is walking his dog when he notices a policeman cuffing a teen and barking at him for breaking curfew. The man walks up to the officer and asks, "Why are you giving that kid a hard time? There is still time left for him to get home before curfew." The officer looks at the man and replies, "There's less than fifteen minutes left, and I know this kid. He lives about twenty minutes from here."

✻ A TEEN IS CAUGHT SMOKING pot behind a local convenience store. He's arrested and put in county jail. The arresting officer advises the young pothead that he gets one phone call from jail. The teen makes his phone call and returns to his cell. About a half hour later a man shows up at the police station. "I assume you're the boy's father," the arresting officer says.

"No," responds the man, "I'm here to deliver a pizza."

✻ TWO YOUNG GIRLS, STUDENTS AT an exclusive prep school in California, are eating lunch and flipping through a celebrity magazine.

"Oh my god, I forgot to tell you!" the blonde says to the brunette. "My mom is getting remarried!"

"No way," the brunette replies. "To who?"

The blonde flips open the magazine and points to a famous director.

"Oh!" screams the brunette. "You'll love him! He was my dad last year!"

 Famous Funnies

"Any kid will run any errand for you, if you ask at bedtime."—Red Skelton

✻ A MOTHER AND SON ARE listening to a special speaker in church. The speaker is recounting the events of his life and says, "The most important piece of advice I ever received was from my mother. Every day, on my way out the door, she'd say to me 'Always remember who you are,' and that advice carried with me through the rest of my life." After the speech, on the ride home, the mother asks her son if there is anything she's told him that stuck with him.

"Yep," the boy replies. "I always remember to bring you the change."

✳ A FATHER PASSING BY HIS son's bedroom is astonished to see that the bed is nicely made and everything is picked up. Then he sees an envelope, propped up prominently on the pillow. It is addressed, "Dad." Fearing the worst, he opens the envelope and reads the letter, with trembling hands. "Dear Dad. It is with great regret and sorrow that I'm writing you. I had to elope with my new girlfriend, because I wanted to avoid a scene with Mom and you. I've been finding real passion with Stacy. She is so nice, but I knew you would not approve of her because of all her piercings and tattoos, her tight motorcycle clothes, and because she is so much older than I am. But it's not only the passion, Dad. She's pregnant. Stacy said that we will be very happy. She owns a trailer in the woods, and has a stack of firewood for the whole winter. We share a dream of having many more children.

"Stacy has opened my eyes to the fact that marijuana doesn't really hurt anyone. We'll be growing it for ourselves and trading it with the other people in the commune for all the cocaine and ecstasy we want. In the meantime, we'll pray that science will find a cure for her disease so that Stacy can get better. She sure deserves it!

"Don't worry, Dad, I'm fifteen, and I know how to take care of myself. Someday, I'm sure we'll be back to visit so you can get to know your many grandchildren. Love, your son, Joshua." The father clutches his heart in pain, but notices more writing on the bottom of the note. "P.S." the letter continues, "Dad, none of the above is true. I'm over at Jason's house. I just wanted to remind you that there are worse things in life than the school report that's on the kitchen table. Call when it is safe for me to come home!"

✳ A FRESHMAN IS TALKING TO the new girl in school. "You'll like it here," he tells her. "Everyone is pretty chill, the teachers are all nice, but the principal is kind of a moron."

"Do you know who I am?" the girl asks her new classmate. "I'm the daughter of the principal."

The boy is silent and then asks her, "Do you know who I am?"

She shakes her head no. "Good," says the boy as he walks away.

✳ A WOOD-SHOP TEACHER VISITS THE workbench of his worst student. "What are you making today?" the teacher asks.

"It's a portable," the student replies.

"A portable what?" the teacher asks. The student answers, "I don't know, I'm still working on the handle."

✳ A TEACHER ASKS HER STUDENT where the English Channel is located. "I'm not sure," the student answers, "we switched cable companies last month."

✳ AN ENGLISH TEACHER TELLS HER class on the first day of school there are two words she will not tolerate in her class. "One is 'gross' and the other is 'awesome.'" A student in the back of the room calls out, "Okay, so what are the words?"

✳ A HIGH SCHOOL CLASS FINISHES a group photo for the high school yearbook. The photo is available for purchase and the teacher is encouraging the class to buy the photo. "Just think about how nice it will be to look back at the photo in twenty years and say, 'Hey, remember Mike? He's a lawyer' or 'Hey, there's Jennifer. She's the top doctor in the region now.'" A student from the back of the class chimes in, "Or, 'Hey, there's the teacher. She's dead.'"

✳ THE TEENAGE SON OF A pastor asks his father to borrow his car. The pastor agrees, if his son will cut his long hair. "What about Sampson? How about Moses? Even Jesus. They all had long hair," the son argues. "You're right," the pastor admits, "and they also walked everywhere."

✱ A FATHER GOES INTO HIS son's room to find him lying face-down on the bed. He asks him, "Hey buddy, how did your test go today?"

"I did just what George Washington did," the son replies, his words muffled by the mattress.

"How so?" the father asks.

The son looks up and answers, "I went down in history."

 ## Famous Funnies

"When I was ten, my family moved to Downers Grove, Illinois. When I was twelve, I found them."—Emo Philips

✱ TEENS ARE AT AN AWKWARD STAGE IN their lives. They know how to make phone calls; they just don't know how to end them.

✱ A TEEN GETS PULLED OVER for speeding. The cop says, "License and registration please." As the teenager is grabbing the registration out of the glove compartment, the cop says, "You know, I've been waiting for a stupid kid like you all day."

The teenager says, "Well officer, I got here as quick as I could."

✱ A TEACHER IS LECTURING HER high school class on how blood circulates through the body. She wants to make sure her class understands, so she asks, "What would happen if I stood on my head? Where would all of the blood go?" A student up front raises her hand and replies that all of the blood would rush to her head. The teacher asks the class, "Then why aren't my feet always red when I'm standing straight up?" A boy in the back responds, "Because your feet aren't as empty as your head."

✱ A FATHER AND MOTHER SEND their son to a special tutor because he's falling behind in school. After weeks of personal classes and hundreds of dollars, the parents ask the tutor for a progress report.

"Good news," the tutor tells them over the phone, "your son is getting straight A's."

"That's outstanding!" says the father.

"I'll say," the tutor replies. "I think we're finally ready to move on to the letter B."

✻ WHAT'S THE DIFFERENCE BETWEEN A teen and E.T.? E.T. actually phoned home.

✻ HOW MANY TEENS DOES IT take to screw in a light bulb? One. He holds the bulb up and the world revolves around him.

Grandparents

✻ GRANDMA AND GRANDPA ARE TRYING to console Susie, whose dog, Skipper, has died. "You know," Grandma says, "it's not so bad. Skipper's probably up in heaven right now, having a grand old time with God." Susie stops crying and asks, "What would God want with a dead dog?"

✻ A YOUNG BOY IS VISITING yard sales with his grandfather. During the ride from one yard sale to the other, the grandfather explains the fine art of haggling. "Here's how it works. Let's say you see something you like for twenty dollars. You make a low offer like ten dollars. They'll probably say no but suggest a price lower than twenty dollars. Then you can make a deal." The young boy says he understands and will give it a shot at the next yard sale. Sure enough, the boy finds a stack of comic books he wants. The comics are priced at five dollars.

"I've only got three dollars," the boy says. "Would you take three dollars for the stack?"

The older woman running the yard sale says, "Sure, for you, I'll make it three dollars."

"Great!" the young boy replies. "Oh, and can you break a ten?"

✳ ON A VISIT TO SEE his grandmother, a teen boy listens as she goes on and on about the cost of living. "When I was a young girl," she moans, "you could go to the store with a dollar and come home with enough food to feed your family for weeks!"

"Well, Grandma," the boy replies, "we learned about that in school recently, and that's called inflation."

"Inflation nothing!" the grandmother answers. "It's all these darn security cameras they've got today!"

✳ A MAN GOES TO VISIT his ninety-year-old grandfather. While eating the eggs and bacon that were prepared for him, he notices a film-like substance on his plate. So he says, "Grandfather, are these plates clean?"

His grandfather replies, "Those plates are as clean as cold water can get them, so go on and finish your meal."

That afternoon, while eating the hamburgers his grandfather made for lunch, he notices many little black specks around the edge of his plate, so again he asks, "Grandfather, are you sure these plates are clean?"

Without looking up from his burger, the grandfather says, "I told you those dishes are as clean as cold water can get them. Now don't ask me about it anymore."

Later that day, as the man is leaving the house, the grandfather's dog, who is lying on the floor, starts to growl and will not let him pass.

"Grandfather, your dog won't let me out," says the grandson.

Without diverting his attention from the football game he's watching, the grandfather shouts, "Coldwater, get out of the way!"

✳ TED'S GRANDMOTHER PULLS HIM ASIDE at his eighth birthday party and hands the boy a five-dollar bill. "Here, this is a little something extra from Grandma. But not a word of this to your brothers and sisters."

The boy looks at the bill and responds, "If you want me to stay quiet it's going to cost you a lot more."

✳ A HUSBAND AND WIFE ARE staring at their garden. "Sooner or later," the wife comments, "you're going to have to put in a better scarecrow."

"What's wrong with the one we've got?" asks the husband. "It scares away all the birds and it's still got a few good years left."

"I agree," the wife says, "but my mother can't stay out there forever."

✳ AN ELDERLY WOMAN GOES TO her local doctor's office and asks to speak with her doctor. When the receptionist asks why she is there, she replies, "I'd like to have some birth control pills." Taken aback, the doctor thinks for a minute and then says, "Excuse me, Mrs. Glenn, but you're eighty years old. What would you possibly need birth control pills for?"

The woman replies, "They help me sleep better."

The doctor considers this for a second, then asks, "How in the world do birth control pills help you sleep?"

The woman says, "I put them in my granddaughter's orange juice, and I sleep better at night."

✳ HOW MANY JEWISH GRANDMOTHERS DOES it take to screw in a light bulb? None, because "never mind us, we'll just sit here in the dark, don't go out of your way . . ."

✳ A GRANDSON GETS INTO AN argument with his grandfather about his generation being much better than the old man's. The grandson explains it is impossible for his grandfather to even understand his generation. "You grew up in a different world," the boy explains. "You didn't have anything and we have everything. Today we have television, jet planes, space travel, man has walked on the moon, and spaceships have visited Mars. We have nuclear energy, electric and hydrogen cars, computers with light-speed processing, and countless other modern advances. You didn't have those things when you were young." "You're right," says the grandfather. "We didn't have those things when we were young—so we invented them!"

✱ "HI! MY NAME IS GERTRUDE," says the lady to the man next to her on the airplane. "It's so nice to meet you! I'm flying to New York for my grandson's third birthday. I'm so excited! I remember when he was just a little pumpkin and now he's already three! It's really hard to believe. He's the most adorable thing you've ever seen! You know what? Hold on, I think I might have a picture on me. Let me take a look in my purse, yes, here it is, just look at him, isn't he adorable? Do you see his dimple on his left cheek? Simply adorable! I could stare at his picture all day. Oh my, and you should hear him on the phone! He is just the cutest, he says to me in the cutest voice 'Hi Grandma!' It just gets me all teary-eyed." After what seems like two hours for the poor man sitting next to her, Gertrude realizes that perhaps she is talking a bit too much.

"You know, I feel terrible! Here I am just talking and talking without letting you get a word in edgewise! Tell me, what do you think about my grandson?"

✱ A YOUNG BOY FINDS HIS grandfather, an avid gardener, working in his garden one afternoon. "What do you usually put on your celery?" the boy asks his grandfather. The old man wipes the sweat and dirt from his forehead. He's amazed his grandson has taken such an interest in his hobby. "Well, I usually put on a mix of enriched soil and rotted horse manure." "That's weird," the grandson replies. "We usually just put on ranch dressing."

✱ A FAMILY MOVES INTO THEIR new house. Grandma comes for a visit and asks the youngest child, a five-year-old, how he likes the new place. "It's terrific," he says. "I have my own room, my brother has his own room, and my sister has her own room. But poor Mom is still sleeping with Dad."

✱ A LITTLE BOY IS LOST at a large shopping mall. He approaches a uniformed security guard and says, "I've lost my grandpa."

The guard asks, "What's he like?"

"Jack Daniel's and *Matlock* reruns," the boy replies.

✳ AN OLD ITALIAN MAN IS dying. He calls his grandson to his bedside and says, "Guido, I want you to listen to me. I want you to take my chrome-plated revolver so you will always remember me."

"But Grandpa," Guido says. "I really don't like guns. How about you leave me your Rolex watch instead?"

"You listen to me. Someday you're gonna run the business. You're gonna have a beautiful wife, a lot of money, a big home, and maybe a couple of bambinos. Someday you're gonna come home and maybe find your wife in bed with another man. What are you gonna do then? Point to your watch and say, 'time's up'?"

✳ A TEENAGE GRANDDAUGHTER COMES DOWNSTAIRS for her date in a see-through top and no bra. Her grandmother goes crazy and tells her she can't go out dressed the way she is. The teenager says, "Loosen up, Grandma! These are modern times. You gotta let your rosebuds show!" And out the door she goes. The next day the teen comes downstairs and finds the grandmother sitting in her favorite chair topless. The teenager is mortified. She explains to her grandmother that she has friends coming over and that it is just not appropriate. The grandmother says, "Loosen up, sweetie. If you can show off your rosebuds, then I can display my hanging baskets."

✳ A GRANDFATHER IS DRIVING HIS three young grandchildren for ice cream on a warm summer evening when a topless woman in a convertible drives by slowly and waves. The six-year-old boy in the back seat is shocked and yells to his grandfather, "Pop-Pop, did you see that crazy woman? She wasn't wearing her seat belt!"

✳ LITTLE BILLY IS SITTING ON a park bench munching on one candy bar after another. After the sixth candy bar, a man on the bench across from him comments, "Son, you know eating all that candy isn't good for you. It will give you acne, rot your teeth, and make you fat."

Little Billy replies, "My grandfather lived to be 107 years old."

"Oh?" replies the man. "Did your grandfather eat six candy bars at a time?"

"No," replies Little Billy. "But he knew when to mind his own business or else."

✷ AN OLD MAN AND WOMAN hate each other, but remain married for years. During their shouting fights, the old man constantly warns his wife, "If I die first, I will dig my way up and out of the grave to come back and haunt you for the rest of your life!" One day, the man abruptly dies. After the burial, the wife goes straight to the local bar and begins to party. Her friends ask if she is worried about her husband digging himself out of the grave. The wife smiles. "Let the old bugger dig. I had him buried upside down!"

CHAPTER 3

Love and Marriage

Frank Sinatra sang, "Love and marriage, love and marriage, it's an institute you can't disparage." Old blue-eyes was half right. It might be difficult to make jokes about love, but you can make jokes about marriage, because there is plenty of material.

Dating

✳ A MAN STOPS BY A florist's shop to buy flowers for his new girlfriend. He asks the proprietor, "You know the expression, 'you should say it with flowers'?"

"How about three dozen of my finest roses?" the florist asks.

"Make it a half dozen roses," the man answers. "I'm a man of very few words."

✳ ON A BUSINESS TRIP, DAVID buys a set of expensive kitchen knives for his girlfriend because her set has grown dull over the years.

His coworker is shocked at the gift. "If you buy her a gift that expensive," he says, "she's going to think you did something wrong on the trip. Maybe cheated or something."

"If I cheated on her," David says, "the last thing I'd buy her is a set of kitchen knives."

✳ A JEALOUS BOYFRIEND CATCHES HIS girlfriend whispering quietly into her cell phone very late one night. "Are you cheating?" her angry boyfriend asks. "Is there somebody else?" The girlfriend laughs and replies, "Do you really think I'd still be dating you if there were someone else?"

 Famous Funnies

> "When you're in love, it's the most glorious two and a half days of your life."—Richard Lewis

✳ STEVE IS WALKING AT THE beach and sees Ollie looking sad and dejected. "What's wrong?" he asks.

"Oh, I tell ya, Steve . . . I've been working out, swimming at the beach here. I just can't get the women to notice me."

Steve nods. "You know, Ollie, I hear there's a trick you can use. You take a potato and put it in your swimming trunks. I hear that makes the girls take notice."

Ollie nods. "By golly, I'll give that a try!"

The next day, Steve sees Ollie at the beach, still sad. "Ah, Steve," he sighs, "I tried that potato thing. It just didn't work."

Steve looks at him and says: "You know, Ollie, the potato is supposed to go in the front."

✳ JAKE BUMPS INTO HIS OLD girlfriend at a coffee shop. "I'm not an accountant anymore," he tells her as they both sip their brews. "I actually gave it all up to be a writer."

"That's amazing," she says. "Have you sold anything?"

"I sure have," he says. "I sold my car, my house, the boat . . ."

✳ TWO MEN ARE COMPLAINING ABOUT their girlfriends not wanting to make love as much anymore.

"We have sex almost every night," the first man says.

"That doesn't sound that bad," the second man says. "Why are you complaining?" "Almost on Monday, almost on Tuesday, almost on . . ."

 ## Comedy Facts

Perhaps the toughest form of comedy to pull off, deadpan comedy is the act of telling jokes without any noticeable change in facial expression or emotion. Also known as dry humor, the key to the performance is in the delivery. Popular deadpan comics of today include Demetri Martin, Todd Barry, and Jonathan Katz.

✱ "I DON'T WANT TO COME off sounding like a jerk," the millionaire says to his date over dessert, "but are you the type of woman who marries a man for money?"

She takes a bite of her cake and answers, "I am, but don't worry, I wouldn't marry you for all the money in the world."

✱ A YOUNG WOMAN IS TALKING online with a man she met in a chat room. After weeks of talking, he asks for a photo of her. She sends her favorite, but prefaces it with, "Remember, the camera adds ten pounds."

He writes back, "I've heard that, and you should stop eating cameras."

✱ TWO SINGLE WOMEN ARE COMPLAINING about their love lives and being generally unlucky in love. "Did you hear about Danielle?" one friend says to the other. "She was in a really bad bike accident. She almost lost a leg. It was saved by the doctor and she actually fell in love with the guy. They are getting married next month."

"Man, that's unreal," the friend says. "Why can't something like that happen to us?"

Comedy Facts

Television is considered the original killer of music hall comedy and entertainment. A music hall performer, or stand-up, could work for years with just one single act. Television created a constant demand for new material and new acts, and performers who couldn't keep up faded away.

✳ A MAN IS OUT ON a date with a woman he met in the grocery store. "Have you been married before?" the woman asks her companion as they wait for drinks to arrive.

Actually," he says, "I've been married twice before. Both of my wives died."

"Oh my. That's terrible. Are you all right talking about it?"

"Yes, I'm fine," the man answers. "Both were very tragic."

"What happened?" she asks, putting her hand on top of his on the table.

"My first wife died from eating poisonous mushrooms," the man explains, "and my second wife was shot."

"That's awful," the woman consoles.

"I'll say," he answers. "She really wouldn't listen when I told her she'd be better off just eating the mushrooms."

✳ ON THEIR FIRST DATE, A young bachelor takes his upstairs neighbor out for drinks.

"What would you like to drink?" he asks, calling over the waitress.

"I'll have champagne, I guess," his date says.

"Um, guess again," the guy replies.

✳ A GIRL INVITES HER DATE into her house at the end of the evening. She still lives with her parents, so she asks the guy to be very quiet when going into the house. On the way to her room, he says he has to use the bathroom.

"This sounds terrible, but you'll have to use the kitchen sink," she says in a whisper. "The only bathroom in the house is right next to their bedroom."

The girl waits in the living room as her date takes care of business in the kitchen. After some time, she stands in the doorway of the kitchen to check on him.

"Everything okay in there?" she whispers into the dark kitchen.

"Yes, everything is fine," her date answers, "but would you mind grabbing me some toilet paper?"

 Famous Funnies

"Men are liars. We'll lie about lying if we have to. I'm an algebra liar. I figure two good lies make a positive." —Tim Allen

✳ A YOUNG MAN SHOWED UP to his date's house and told her they were going to have "an awesome time" that evening. "What are we doing?" she asked.

"I got three tickets to a concert."

"Why would we need three tickets?" his date asked.

"The tickets are for your parents and sister."

✳ A MAN IS DRIVING UP a steep, narrow mountain road. His ex-girlfriend is driving down the same road. As they pass each other, the woman leans out of the window and yells, "PIG!" The man immediately leans out of his window and replies, "WITCH!" They each continue on their way, and as the man rounds the next corner, he crashes into a pig in the middle of the road.

✳ A GIRLFRIEND BETS HER INVENTOR boyfriend that he can't make a car out of nothing but ravioli. You should have seen her face when he drove right pasta.

✳ THE TROUBLE WITH WOMEN IS that they tend to get excited over almost nothing—and then they marry him.

 Joke Essentials

There will be some jokes you'll tell repeatedly, which is fine, because you begin to give those jokes a personal rhythm. The more you tell the joke, the more refined that rhythm becomes. A joke's rhythm is measured not by the words, but by the timing of its delivery.

✳ ONE EVENING A MAN WALKS into a fast-food chicken place and buys a nine-piece bucket of chicken. He takes his chicken to the park for a romantic dinner under the moonlight with his lady. Upon reaching into the bucket, however, he receives a surprise. Instead of chicken, he discovers what is apparently the restaurant's night deposit—some nine thousand bucks. The young man takes the bucket back to the store and asks for his chicken in exchange for the money. The manager, in awe of the young man's honesty, asks for his name and tells him he wants to call the newspaper and the local news station to do a story on him. He will become a local hero, an example of honesty and morality that would inspire others! The hungry man shrugs it off. "My date's waiting. I just want my chicken."

The manager's amazement over the young man's humility almost overwhelms him. He begs to be allowed to tell the story on the news. At this, the honest man becomes angry with the manager and demands his chicken.

"I don't get it," the manager responds. "You are an honest man in a dishonest world! This is a perfect opportunity to show the world that there are honest people still willing to take a stand for what is right. Please, give me your name and also the woman's name. Is that your wife?"

"That's the problem," says the young man. "My wife is at home. The woman in the car is my girlfriend. Now let me have my chicken so I can get out of here."

✳ SEEING THE NAME OF TWO lovers carved into a tree is kind of charming at first, but then really creepy when you think about how many people bring knives on dates.

✳ AFTER TRAVELING ON BUSINESS, TIM thinks it would be nice to bring his girlfriend a little gift. "How about some perfume?" he asks the cosmetics clerk. She shows him a fifty-dollar bottle.

"That's a bit much," says Tim, so she returns with a smaller bottle for thirty dollars.

"That's still quite a bit," Tim complains. Growing annoyed, the clerk brings out a tiny fifteen-dollar bottle.

"What I mean," says Tim, "is I'd like to see something really cheap." So the clerk hands him a mirror.

✳ WHY DO PEPPERS MAKE BAD girlfriends? Because they are constantly jalapeño business.

✳ A TEEN BOY CALLS 911. "Help," he yells into the phone, "there's an emergency. Two girls from my school are fighting over me."

"So what's the emergency?" asks the 911 operator.

The boy shouts over the line, "The ugly one is winning!"

✳ A BOSS IS AT WORK one day and notices that a long-time employee is wearing a small hoop earring. The employee is usually an incredibly conservative fellow, and the boss is curious about his sudden change in fashion choices. The boss walks up to him at lunch and says, "I didn't know you were into earrings."

"It's not really a big deal, it's only an earring," the employee replies, embarrassed.

"How long have you been wearing one?" the boss asks.

"Ever since I told my girlfriend it was mine after she found it in our bed."

✳ A YOUNG MAN MEETS AN attractive woman at a bar. After a few drinks, they end up back at her condo. They make passionate love all night long and the man spends the night. The next morning, getting dressed, he notices a framed photo of an attractive young man on her dresser. Worried it might be a jealous husband or boyfriend, he asks her, "Who's the guy in the picture?"

"Oh," she replies, still lying in bed, "that was me before the surgery."

✳ AN ASPIRING ACTOR WANTS TO marry his girlfriend. He goes to her father to ask his permission for her to marry. "I could never let my daughter marry an actor," the father responds.

"But you've never even seen me act," cries the actor. "How about this—you come see me perform and then you give me your decision."

The father agrees and goes to a performance the following evening. After the show ends, the young actor meets his girlfriend's father in the audience.

"I've changed my mind about letting you marry my daughter," the father says. "After seeing your performance tonight I realized that you're no actor."

 Joke Essentials

Always evaluate the material. Evaluate jokes you're currently telling, and after telling a particular joke, ask yourself, "Did that joke work?" Be honest, and if it's working (getting a few laughs), keep telling it. If not, don't waste time on unfunny material.

✳ A POLICE OFFICER FINDS A young couple messing around in their parked car. The officer shines his light into the window. The young man jumps out of the car and claims, "Honest, officer, we weren't doing anything."

"In that case," the officer replies, "let me inside and you come out and hold the flashlight."

✳ BILL TAKES HIS DATE TO an exclusive restaurant on their first date. To impress her, Bill orders the entire meal in French. She is impressed. The waiters are very impressed, but very also confused, since it is a Chinese restaurant.

✳ WHILE VISITING A FRIEND IN the hospital, a young man notices several gorgeous nurses, each one of them wearing a pin designed to look like an apple. "What does the pin signify?" he asks one of them.

"Oh, nothing," she says with a chuckle. "We just use it to keep the doctors away."

✳ A MAN CHEATS ON HIS girlfriend, Lorraine, with a girl named Clearly. Suddenly, Lorraine dies. At the funeral, the man stands up and sings loudly, "I can see Clearly now, Lorraine is gone."

✳ HOW IS BEING AT A singles bar different from going to the circus? At the circus the clowns don't talk.

✳ A YOUNG WOMAN IN NEW York is so depressed that she decides to end her life by throwing herself into the ocean. She goes down to the docks and is about to leap into the frigid water when a handsome young sailor sees her tottering on the edge of the pier, crying. He takes pity on her and says, "Look, you have so much to live for. I'm off to Europe in the morning, and if you like, I can stow you away on my ship. I'll take good care of you and bring you food every day." Moving closer, he slips his arm around her shoulder and adds, "I'll keep you happy, and you'll keep me happy." The girl nods yes. After all, what does she have to lose? Perhaps a fresh start in Europe will give her life new meaning.

That night, the sailor brings her aboard and hides her in a lifeboat. From then on, every night he brings her three sandwiches and a piece of fruit, and they make passionate love until dawn. Three weeks later, during a routine inspection, she is discovered by the captain. "What are you doing here?" the captain asks.

"I have an arrangement with one of the sailors," she explains. "I get food and a trip to Europe, and he's screwing me."

"He certainly is," the captain says. "This is the Staten Island Ferry."

✳ JACK WANTS TO GET MARRIED, but his mother hates every girl he brings home. A friend suggests finding a woman exactly like his mother. After an exhaustive search, Jack finds a woman who dresses like his mother, cooks like his mother, makes jokes like his mother, and even looks like his mother did when she was young. His mother loves her from the moment they meet. He tells his friend everything the next time they hang out.

"So, what's the next step?" his friend asks.

"Well, I'm dating again," Jack admits. "I had to dump her because my father hated her guts."

✳ A BRIDE WALKS DOWN THE aisle at her wedding and, upon reaching the altar, finds that the groom is standing next to his golf bag. The bride whispers to her husband-to-be, "What are your golf clubs doing here?"

He looks her in the eyes and replies, "This isn't going to take all day, is it?"

 Famous Funnies

"Behind every great man is a woman rolling her eyes."—Jim Carrey

✳ AN ENGINEER CROSSES A ROAD when a frog calls out to him, "If you kiss me, I'll turn into a beautiful princess." He bends over, picks up the frog, and puts it in his pocket. The frog speaks up again and says, "If you kiss me and turn me back into a beautiful princess, I will stay with you for one week." The engineer takes the frog out of his pocket, smiles at it, and returns it to the pocket. The frog then cries out, "If you kiss me and turn me back, I'll do whatever you say!" Again the engineer takes the frog out, smiles at it, and puts it back into his pocket. Finally, the frog asks, "What is the matter? I've told you I'm a beautiful princess, I'll stay with you for a month, and do whatever you say. What more do you want?"

The engineer says, "Look, I'm an engineer. I don't have time for a girlfriend, but a talking frog? Now that's cool!"

❋ TODD AND JESSICA ARE ON a blind date. Todd picks up Jessica at her house and asks her, "What would you like to do first?" Jessica replies enthusiastically, "Get weighed!" Confused, Todd takes her to a pharmacy and lets her weigh herself on the scale inside. He suggests going to get a bite to eat. After dinner he asks her again what she'd like to do. "Get weighed!" Jessica again blurts out. So Todd takes her back to the pharmacy a second time. They go to see a late movie and Todd asks her one more time what to do for the evening. "Get weighed!" she exclaims one last time. Tired of taking her to the pharmacy, Todd takes her back to her place and says goodnight.

"How was your date?" Jessica's roommate asks as she walks through the front door.

"Wousy!" Jessica replies.

 Joke Essentials

No one has a perfect memory. You'll forget almost as many jokes as you remember. Keep a joke file. Put all of your favorite jokes in a journal, on index cards, or in a document on your computer. It helps to remember old jokes you've forgotten over the years.

❋ A BOYFRIEND AND GIRLFRIEND ENTER a dentist's office. The girlfriend says, "I need a tooth pulled. No gas or Novocain—I'm in a terrible hurry. Just pull the tooth as quickly as possible."

"You're a brave woman," says the dentist. "Now, show me which tooth it is."

The girlfriend turns to her boyfriend and says, "Open your mouth and show the dentist which tooth it is, babe."

✴ THE BEST PART ABOUT DATING a homeless woman is that when the evening comes to an end, you can really drop her off anywhere.

✴ DID YOU HEAR ABOUT THE attractive girl dating the guy with the wooden leg? When she found out, she broke it off.

✴ A YOUNG GUY GOES TO the house of the girl he's dating. It's his first time over. She shows him around the house and leaves him in the living room while she goes to the kitchen to get some drinks. The guy notices a small vase alone on the mantel. He picks it up and is looking it over just as the girl comes back into the room with the drinks.

"What's this?" the guy asks, holding up the vase.

"Oh, those are my father's ashes."

The guy returns the vase to its proper spot and apologizes. "I'm so sorry, I had no idea."

"It's okay," she says. "It's just that he's too lazy to go to the kitchen to get an ashtray."

✴ NEVER DATE A RADIOLOGIST. SHE'LL see right through you.

✴ TWO OLD PEOPLE FLIRT AT a singles bar. After a few drinks, the old man asks the old woman, "If I took you out for a full night of wining, dining, and dancing, what would you wear?"

The old woman replies shyly, "Depends."

"Depends on what?" he asks.

"On my bottom—where else?"

Marriage

✴ WHAT WAS ADAM AND EVE'S biggest problem during their marriage? They could never agree on who wore the plants in the family.

✻ A WOMAN IS HAVING LUNCH in a Los Angeles cafe when a man approaches her table. "Excuse me, miss," the man says, "my wife and I are visiting from out of town. She loves your sandals. She wanted me to come over and ask if you bought those sandals around here."

"Actually," the woman responds, "I got them in a shop just about a block from here."

"Fantastic," the man responds, "and if I may ask, how much did you pay for them?"

"I paid $250," she admits.

"Thank you," the man responds. He walks away and yells to his wife, "She got them in New York!"

✻ ONE SUNDAY MORNING, SATAN APPEARS before a small-town congregation. Everyone starts screaming and running for the front church door, trampling each other in a frantic effort to get away. Soon, everyone is gone, except for an elderly gentleman who sits calmly. Satan walks up to the man and says, "Don't you know who I am?"

The man replies, "I sure do."

Satan asks, "Aren't you going to run away like the others?"

"Nope, no reason to," says the man.

Angry, Satan asks, "Why aren't you afraid of me?"

The man calmly replies, "I've been married to your sister for more than forty-eight years."

✻ A HUSBAND AND WIFE ARE in line at the grocery store. The clerk asks if they have a preferred shopper's card.

"Yes," says the wife, "but I left it at home."

The clerk says he can look it up by birthday. The woman gives her birthday, but he can't find her card in the system. After a few more tries, he asks her for more information, until her account finally comes up on the computer.

"I think I see the issue," the clerk says. "Someone put your birthday in the system as 6/24/1899."

"Obviously, that's wrong," the woman says.

The husband finally breaks his silence and adds, "She was born in September of that year, not June."

✱ AN OLD WOMAN IS TELLING her friend a story over the phone. She gets one of the details wrong and her husband, overhearing the call, corrects her mistake. "We've been married fifty-seven years," the woman says, "and you're still correcting me every chance you get."

The man nods his head in agreement and adds, "We've been married fifty-eight years."

✱ A WIFE COMES DOWN WITH the flu and needs her husband to do her chores around the house. She knows he'll put up a fight, even with her sick, so she decides to try some reverse psychology.

"Honey, I'm feeling terrible. What I'm really feeling terrible about is leaving all the dishes dirty, the bed unmade, and the house a complete mess."

"Don't you worry about that," the husband says. "You just rest up and get better. It will all be there for you to do when you feel up to it."

✱ AFTER OPEN HEART SURGERY, A man is instructed by his doctor to change a few things in his life if he wants to live to an old age.

"Your heart is fragile," the doctor explains. "So you've got to cut out smoking, drinking, and red meats."

"What about sex?" the man asks.

"Sex is fine," the doctor says, "but only with your wife. We don't want you getting too excited."

✱ TWO WOMEN ARE DISCUSSING THEIR husbands. The first woman says that she thinks the other woman's husband is cheating.

"He's constantly lying to you," the first woman says. "Do you really think he went fishing last weekend? He didn't come home with a single fish."

"Well," says the second woman, "that's kind of the reason I believe him."

✸ A WOMAN RETURNS HOME FROM shopping and tells her husband that a car backed into her and caused severe damage. The car sped away before she could write down any information about the vehicle.

"Well, do you at least remember what type of car it was?"

"I have no idea," the woman says. "I don't know the first thing about cars."

For weeks, the husband points out every single car on the road. He tells her the make and model until she can finally name every single car on the road. She comes home excited from shopping one weekend to happily report, "Honey, I hit a BMW 760Li!"

Joke Essentials

Sometimes called trebling, the "Rule of Three" is a pattern used in jokes where part of the story is repeated three times, but with minor variations each time. The first two instances build tension while the third releases the tension by incorporating a twist. Most jokes follow the Rule of Three, except for one-liners.

✸ A YOUNG COUPLE ARE TRYING to save money on their summer vacation. They bring their bags to the discount airline desk to check in.

"Do you have reservations?" asks the woman behind the counter.

"More than a few," the young man answers, "but we're flying with you guys anyway."

✸ A COUPLE IS SITTING ON the porch sipping wine. The wife says, "I love you."

The husband says, "Is that you or the wine talking?"

The wife replies, "It's me, talking to the wine."

✳ A WIFE GOES TO THE police station with her next-door neighbor to report that her husband is missing. The policeman asks for a description. She says, "He's thirty-five years old, six foot four, has dark eyes, dark wavy hair, an athletic build, weighs 185 pounds, is soft-spoken, and is good to the children."

The next-door neighbor protests, "Your husband is five foot four, chubby, bald, has a big mouth, and is mean to your children."

The wife replies, "Yes, but who wants *him* back?"

✳ A DRIVER IS STOPPED BY a police officer. The driver asks, "What's the problem, officer?"

"You were going at least seventy-five in a fifty-five zone," the officer replies.

"No sir, I was going sixty-five," the man protests.

"Oh, Harry. You were going at least eighty," his wife says.

"I'm also going to give you a ticket for your broken taillight," the cop adds.

"Broken taillight? I didn't know about a broken taillight!" the man protests.

"Oh, Harry," the wife chimes in, "you've known about that taillight for weeks."

"I'm also going to give you a citation for not wearing your seat belt," the officer adds.

"I just took it off when you were walking up to the car!" the man screams.

"Oh, Harry, you never wear your seat belt," his wife piles on. The man turns to his wife and yells, "Would you please shut up!"

The officer leans into the window and says to the wife, "Ma'am, does your husband talk to you this way all the time?"

The wife replies, "No, officer, only when he's drunk."

✳ EARLY IN THE MORNING, A wife turns over to find her husband wide awake in bed.

"Are you okay?" the wife asks.

"I guess," he replies.

"I'm asking because you spent the entire night cursing me in your sleep."

The man replies, "Who said I was asleep?"

✳ A WIFE STANDS MOTIONLESS IN her kitchen, staring into space. Her husband walks in and asks what she is doing. "I came in here for something," she explains, "and now I don't remember what it was. I really think I'm losing my mind."

"That wouldn't surprise me," the husband replies. "You've been giving me a piece of it every day for twenty years."

✳ BILL VISITS HIS FRIEND MIKE at home. Bill immediately notices the way Mike treats his wife. He constantly tells her how much he loves her, hugs and kisses her every time she enters the room, and brags about her to Bill when she is around. "Wow," says Bill after she leaves to grab the men some beers. "You really treat your wife great."

Mike responds, "Yeah, she really pulled me out of a funk about six months ago. I'm really thankful for her. Plus, this new attitude toward her has really changed our marriage."

Inspired by his friend, Bill goes home, grabs his wife, and kisses her passionately.

"My dear," he says, "have I ever told you how much I love and respect you?"

Mike's wife immediately begins to cry. "What's wrong?" he asks.

"Oh, I'm having the worst day! Our son broke his ankle skateboarding, the washing machine is busted, and now to top it all off you come home drunk!"

✳ A GROOM-TO-BE IS HAVING DINNER with his father on the night before his wedding.

"Any last-minute tips about marriage?" he asks his father while waiting for the main course.

"Yes," replies his dad, "I've got two pieces of advice. Set out the rule that you've got to spend at least one night a week hanging out with your friends. The second piece of advice is don't waste that one night a week on your friends."

 Famous Funnies

"My husband and I didn't sign a pre-nuptial agreement. We signed a mutual suicide pact."—Roseanne Barr

* "I'M STARTING TO THINK THE only reason you married me is because my great-aunt left me $10 million," a wife says to her husband during another argument.

"That's absurd," the husband replies. "I wouldn't care who left it to you."

* A DRUNK HUSBAND WAKES UP from another all-night bender and stumbles into the kitchen.

"I'm guessing you feel awful again this morning," his wife snaps.

"Actually, I feel good," the husband responds. "I slept like a log."

"You didn't even come to bed," the wife answers.

"I know," he answers. "I passed out in the fireplace."

* TWO MEN ARE DRINKING AT a bar all night. Finally, one man says to the other, "I hate to break up the fun, but I've got to go home and take off my wife's underwear."

The other man replies, "What makes you think you'll be so lucky?"

The first man replies while walking out the door, "Because they've been riding up my butt all night and I've had enough."

* TWO MEN ARE DISCUSSING THE possible dangers linked with smoking. "I've got one friend who died because his wife smoked," the first explains, "but it was because his wife lit up while filling the car with gas."

✳ A WIFE WALKS INTO A gun shop and asks for help in choosing a rifle. "It's for my husband," the woman tells the clerk.

"Okay," replies the clerk, opening the display case. "Did he mention what caliber rifle he was interested in?"

"No, he didn't," the wife replies. "In fact, he has no idea I'm even planning on shooting him."

✳ A HUSBAND AND WIFE ARE sitting at a table at her twentieth high school reunion. There is an incredibly drunk man slumped over at the table across from them.

"Do you know that guy?" the husband asks.

"Yes," the wife replies somberly. "That's my ex-boyfriend. He started drinking right after we broke up and hasn't been sober since."

"Good God," the husband replies. "Who knew it was possible to celebrate for that long?"

✳ A MAN IS EXPLAINING TO his coworker that he never realized how much his wife loved him until he was home sick from work the previous day.

"Really?" the coworker asks. "What showed you she really loved you?"

"She was just really excited to have me around," the man replies. "Like when the mailman and FedEx guy came to the door she shouted excitedly, 'My husband is home! My husband is home!'"

✳ TWO MEN ARE SITTING IN a sauna after a workout. "I'll be honest, my wife really is an angel."

"You're lucky," the second man answers, wiping the sweat from his brow. "My wife is still alive."

✳ "I CAN'T BELIEVE YOU'RE SLEEPING with my best friend!" a husband yells at his wife while packing up his belongings.

"Does the fact that he finds me attractive really surprise you?" the wife asks.

"Yes," the man replies, "especially after everything I've told him!"

✳ "IT'S REALLY HOT OUTSIDE," A husband tells his wife, staring out the front window. "What do you think the neighbors would think if I mowed the lawn naked?" he asks jokingly.

The wife replies without looking up from the morning paper, "They'll probably think I married you for the money."

✳ A HUSBAND IS READING THE paper while his wife drinks coffee at the kitchen table. "Listen to this," the husband says to his wife. "It says that in an average day a man uses 2,200 words while a woman uses around 5,000. That's more than double!"

The wife, never looking up from her coffee, rebuffs, "That's because women have to tell men everything twice."

✳ A COUPLE IS DRIVING HOME from a party when the wife turns to the husband and says, "Have I ever told you how sexy and irresistible you are to women?"

The man blushes and answers, "No, I don't believe you ever have."

She responds quickly, "Then why on earth did you think that at the party tonight?"

✳ WHAT'S THE DIFFERENCE BETWEEN A pregnant woman and a supermodel? Nothing, if the husband knows what's best for him.

✳ A MARRIED COUPLE IS SHOPPING at Costco. The husband picks up a case of beer and puts it into the cart.

"What do you think you're doing?" the wife asks.

"It's on sale for twenty dollars," the husband explains.

"I don't care," says the wife, "we're on a budget, so put it back."

A couple aisles later the wife puts a fifty-dollar container of face cream in the cart.

"What's that all about?" the husband asks.

"It's my face cream. I use it daily and it's less expensive here. Plus, you should be happy. It keeps me looking beautiful."

The husband answers, "Well, so does the beer, and that's much cheaper."

* A WIFE SENDS HER HUSBAND grocery shopping. He fills two carts with food and gets in line to pay. An old woman gets behind him with just a loaf of bread and gallon of milk. "Excuse me, ma'am," the man turns to ask, "is that all you've got to purchase?"

"Yes," says the old woman.

"Well, you'd better grab a seat, I'm going to be a while," the man tells her.

* A MAN WALKS UP TO the perfume counter of a department store and asks for the most expensive bottle of perfume.

"A surprise gift for the wife?" the clerk asks, wrapping the bottle.

"Yeah," the man replies, "she thinks she's getting tickets for a cruise."

* THE GUEST OF HONOR AT an awards dinner is about to give his speech when a stagehand gives him a piece of paper from his wife in the crowd.

"What does it say?" the stagehand asks.

"Oh, it just says KISS in very big letters."

"Wow, that's very sweet," the stagehand replies. "She must love you and be very proud of you."

"Not really," the man says. "It stands for Keep It Short, Stupid."

* A WIFE SAYS TO HER husband, "Just once, I'd like you to experience what it's like to be a woman." The husband says okay and leaves the house. He comes back forty-five minutes later.

"Where have you been?" the wife asks.

"I've been outside," her husband explains, "trying to park the car."

✳ A HUSBAND IS LATE COMING home one night and isn't answering his cell phone. His wife calls her mother, incredibly upset. "I'm afraid he's having an affair," she tells her mother.

"Why do you always think the worst?" her mother asks. "Maybe he just got in a car crash or something."

✳ TWO WOMEN ARE HAVING COFFEE, complaining about their husbands.

"My husband is only good for one thing," the first woman says.

"I know," the second woman adds, "and how often does parallel parking really come up?"

✳ A MAN IS STAGGERING HOME drunk after last call. A policeman sees the man stumbling around and asks where he's going.

"I'm heading to a lecture," the man slurs in response.

"A lecture?" the skeptical cop responds. "Who would be giving a lecture at this time of the night?"

"My wife," the drunk man answers.

✳ MATT'S WIFE HAS BEEN DROPPING hints about her birthday gift for weeks. Now, on the day before, Matt asks, "So what do you think you're getting for your birthday?"

His wife responds, "All I know is that it better be in the driveway and it better go from zero to 200 in under six seconds."

"Oh, it will," Matt responds, "and it does."

The next morning his wife wakes up to find a bathroom scale in the driveway.

✳ AFTER A LONG NIGHT OF work, a boss and his assistant have a few drinks to celebrate the completion of their presentation. One thing leads to another and the boss and assistant ending up making love on the conference room table. Before the boss knows it, it is 3 A.M.

"Oh man!" he exclaims. "My wife will hang me!"

Thinking quickly, he picks up the phone and dials his house. "Darling! It's me," he whispers breathlessly into the phone. "Don't pay the ransom! I've escaped!"

✳ AN AMISH BOY AND HIS father are visiting a nearby mall. They are amazed by almost everything they see, but especially by two shiny silver walls that move apart and back together again by themselves.

The lad asks, "What is this, Father?"

The father, having never seen an elevator, responds, "I have no idea what it is."

While the boy and his father are watching wide-eyed, an old lady in a wheelchair rolls up to the moving walls and presses a button. The walls open and the lady rolls between them into a small room. The walls close and the boy and his father watch as small circles light up above the walls. The walls open up again and a beautiful twenty-four-year-old woman steps out. The father looks at his son excitedly and says, "Go get your mother."

✳ A WOMAN CALLS HER HUSBAND at work to share some news. "I'm kind of busy right now, babe, can't it wait until I get home?"

"Not really," she replies. "I've just got to share some good news and some bad news." "All right," he replies, playing along. "I'm in a rush, so just give me the good news." "Well," she sighs, "the good news is that the airbags on the car work correctly."

✳ A HUSBAND AND WIFE CELEBRATE being married for fifty years and never getting into an argument. The husband asks his wife, "How did you make it through all those years without getting into an argument?"

The old woman says every time she got mad at her husband, she would sew a doily, and it would calm her down. The next day, the husband and wife are cleaning out a closet and the husband finds a box with one doily and a stack of money totaling $25,000.

He is excited to find the money, but also happy that after all these years, his wife has only gotten mad at him one time.

He asks his wife about the contents of the box. She says, "Well, the doily is from just last week, when you forgot to pick me up from the doctor's office, and the money is from the past fifty years of selling doilies."

✱ TWO MEN ARE TALKING ABOUT their wives after a game of tennis.

"We're going to try to have another kid," the first man says to his friend.

"That's great news!" his friend replies. "When are you going to start trying?"

The first man responds, "As soon as our older son stops sleeping in our bed."

✱ A COUPLE GOES TO SEE a magic show. After the show, the magician meets the crowd for autographs and questions. The husband shakes the hand of the magician and says, "It was a fantastic show. How the heck did you do the trick with the steak knives and pillowcase?"

The magician laughs and says, "I could tell you the secret, but then I'd have to kill you." The man thinks it over for a moment and says, "Fine, then just go ahead and tell my wife."

✱ LARRY GOES TO SEE HIS supervisor in the front office. "Boss," he says, "we're doing some heavy housecleaning at home tomorrow, and my wife needs me to help with the attic and the garage, moving and hauling stuff."

"We're short-handed," the boss replies. "I can't give you the day off."

"Thanks, boss," says Larry, "I knew I could count on you!"

✱ A MAN HATES HIS WIFE'S cat with a passion and decides to get rid of it once and for all. He drives twenty blocks away from home and drops the cat there. The cat is already walking up the driveway as the man approaches his house. The next day, he decides to drop the cat forty blocks away, but the same thing happens. He keeps on increasing the number of blocks, but the cat keeps on coming home before him.

At last he decides to drive a few miles away, turn right, then left, past the bridge, then right again, and another right and so on until he reaches what he thinks is a perfect spot and drops the cat there. Hours later, the man calls his wife at home and asks her, "Jen, is the cat there?"

"Yes, why do you ask?" answers the wife.

Frustrated, the man says, "Put that cat on the phone. I'm lost and I need directions."

* A MARRIED COUPLE LOOKS OVER the side of a wishing well. The guy leans over, makes a wish, and throws in a penny. His wife decides to make a wish, too, but she leans over too far, falls into the well, and drowns. The guy says, "Wow, it really works."

* A MAN GOES INTO A restaurant. He has a seat at a booth and opens a menu to find out that none of the foods have prices next to them. He asks the waiter, "How much is the Fettuccine Alfredo?"

The waiter says, "A penny."

The man exclaims, "A penny? How much for a steak?"

The waiter says, "A nickel." The man is astonished.

"Are you serious? Where's the man who owns this place? I'd like to shake his hand!"

The waiter answers, "He's upstairs with my wife."

Confused, the man asks, "What's he doing upstairs with your wife?"

The waiter smiles and says, "The same thing I'm doing down here to his business."

* THREE WOMEN ARE DISCUSSING THEIR sex lives over coffee. The first woman says, "My husband is an architect. When we have sex he's always erect."

The second woman tells her friends, "My husband is a professional body builder. Our sex is always about power."

The third woman looks up from her coffee and says, "My husband is a computer programmer. When we make love he turns all of the lights off, does nothing for five minutes, and then tells me how great it's going to be when we finally get started."

✳ A PRISONER IN JAIL RECEIVES a letter from his wife: "Dear husband, I have decided to plant some lettuce in the back garden. When is the best time to plant them?" The prisoner, knowing that the prison guards read all mail, replies in a letter: "Dear wife, whatever you do, do not touch the back garden. That is where I hid all the money."

A week or so later, he receives another letter from his wife. "Dear husband, you wouldn't believe what happened. Some men came with shovels to the house and dug up the back garden."

The prisoner writes back: "Dear wife, now is the best time to plant the lettuce."

✳ AFTER THIRTY YEARS OF MARRIAGE a husband and wife go for counseling. When asked what the problem is, the wife goes into a tirade listing every problem they had ever had in the years they had been married. On and on she goes: Neglect, lack of intimacy, emptiness, loneliness, feeling unloved and unlovable—an entire laundry list of unmet needs she has endured. Finally, after allowing this for a sufficient length of time, the therapist gets up, walks around the desk, and after asking the wife to stand, he embraces and kisses her long and passionately as her husband watches with a raised eyebrow. The woman shuts up and quietly sits down as though in a daze. The therapist turns to the husband and says, "This is what your wife needs at least three times a week. Can you do this?"

"Well, I can drop her off here on Mondays and Wednesdays, but on Fridays, I fish."

✱ A MAN IS SITTING AT home when a police officer knocks on his door. The officer asks him if he is married and the man replies, "Yes I am." The officer then asks him if he has a recent picture of his wife. The man answers, "Sure, hold on a second." The officer looks at the picture, and in a sad voice says, "I'm sorry, but it looks like your wife has been hit by a train."

The man says, "I know, but she has a good personality."

✱ A VERY ELDERLY COUPLE IS celebrating their seventy-fifth wedding anniversary. The man says to his wife, "Dear, there is something that I must ask you. It has always bothered me that our tenth child never looked quite like the rest. Now, I want to assure you that these seventy-five years have been the most wonderful experience I could have ever hoped for, and your answer could not take all of that away. But, I must know, did he have a different father?"

The wife drops her head, unable to look her husband in the eye, and then confesses. "Yes, he did."

The old man is very shaken, the reality hitting him harder than he expected. With a tear in his eye he asks, "Who? Who was he? Who was the father?"

Again the woman drops her head, saying nothing at first as she tries to muster the courage to tell the truth to her husband. Then, finally she says to her husband, "You."

✱ THERE ARE THREE RINGS INVOLVED in every marriage—the engagement ring, the wedding ring, and the suffering.

✱ A MAN SPENDS ALL NIGHT drinking in a bar and ends up vomiting all over his shirt. He doesn't know what to do, since he told his wife he would be working late and is worried that if she sees the vomit he'll be caught in a lie. His drinking buddy says, "No worries, just stick a ten-dollar bill in your pocket, and tell your wife some guy puked on you and gave you the money for the cleaning bill!"

So, he goes home to his wife and explains what happened. She then asks, "So why are there two ten-dollar bills in your pocket?"

He replies, "Oh, because the guy peed in my pants too!"

✳ A MAN COMES HOME FROM work, sits down in his favorite chair, turns on the TV, and says to his wife, "Quick, bring me a beer before it starts." She looks a little puzzled, but brings him a beer. When he finishes it, he says, "Quick, bring me another beer. It's gonna start." This time she looks a little angry, but brings him a beer. When he finishes the beer, he calls to her, "Quick, another beer before it starts."

"That's it!" She blows her top. "You jerk. You waltz in here, flop your fat butt down, don't even say hello to me, and then expect me to run around like your slave. Don't you realize that I cook and clean and wash and iron all day long?"

The husband sighs. "Oh man, it started!"

✳ A WOMAN TELLS HER FRIEND she is getting married for the fourth time. "How wonderful! I hope you don't mind my asking, what happened to your first husband?"

"He ate poisonous mushrooms and died."

"Oh, how tragic! What about your second husband?"

"He also ate poisonous mushrooms and died."

"Oh, how terrible! I'm almost afraid to ask you about your third husband."

"He died of a broken neck."

"A broken neck?"

"He wouldn't eat the mushrooms."

✳ A MARRIAGE CERTIFICATE IS A clever way of saying "work permit."

✳ WALKING DOWN THE STREET, A man hears a voice: "Stop! If you take one more step, a brick will fall down and kill you." The man stops; a big brick falls in front of him. The astonished man continues walking to the crosswalk. The voice shouts, "Stop! If you take one more step, a car will run over you and you will die." The man stands still; a car comes careening around the corner, barely missing him. "Where are you?" the man asks. "Who are you?"

"I am your guardian angel," the voice answers.

"Oh yeah?" the man asks. "Where the hell were you when I got married last week?"

✳ AN OLD MAN GOES TO his doctor and says, "I don't think my wife's hearing is as good as it used to be. What should I do?"

The doctor replies, "Try this test to find out for sure. When your wife is in the kitchen doing dishes, stand fifteen feet behind her and ask her a question. If she doesn't respond, keep moving closer, asking the question until she hears you."

The man goes home and sees his wife preparing dinner. He stands fifteen feet behind her and says, "What's for dinner, honey?" No response. He moves to ten feet behind her and asks again—no response. Five feet, no answer. Finally, he stands directly behind her and asks, "Honey, what's for supper?"

She says, "For the fourth time, I said chicken!"

✳ IF A GUY HOLDS A woman's hand when they are dating, he's in love. If he holds her hand during marriage, it's to keep her from punching him.

✳ TELL A WOMAN YOU'D "GO through hell for her" and she'll believe you. Marry her and the trip through hell might become a reality.

✳ A HUSBAND AND WIFE GO to a restaurant. The waiter approaches the table to take their order. "I'll have your biggest, juiciest steak," says the husband.

"But sir, what about the mad cow?" asks the waiter.

"Oh," says the husband, "she'll order for herself."

✳ THERE ARE THREE MEN WORKING on the top of a cliff.

The first says, "If I have cheese in my sandwich tomorrow, I'll jump off this cliff."

The second says, "If I have jam in my sandwich tomorrow, I'll jump off the cliff."

The third says, "If I have ham tomorrow, I'll jump off the cliff."

The next day, the first man has cheese, the second has jam, and the last has ham. So they all jump. At the funerals, the wife of the first man says to the wife of the second, "Why didn't they just tell us they didn't like their sandwiches?"

The wife of the third man says, "I don't know why my husband jumped off the cliff. He made his own sandwiches."

* A MAN IS ON A cross-country trip when he picks up a hitchhiker. During a lull in the conversation, the hitchhiker notices a brown paper bag resting in the center console. The driver notices his glance and says, "That's a bottle of wine. I got it for my wife."

The hitchhiker replies, "That's a pretty good trade."

* REAL MEN WEAR PINK BECAUSE that's what their wives bought.

* A MAN PHONES HOME FROM the office and tells his wife, "Something has just come up. I need to go fishing with the boss for the weekend. We leave right away, so can you pack my clothes, my fishing equipment, and my blue silk pajamas? I'll be home in an hour to pick them up."

He hurries home, grabs everything, and rushes off. Sunday night, he returns. His wife asks, "Did you have a good trip?"

"Oh yes, great! I think I really impressed the boss. But you forgot to pack my blue silk pajamas."

"Oh, no I didn't. I put them in your tackle box."

* TWO BROOMS ARE GETTING MARRIED. Before the ceremony, the bride broom says to the groom broom, "I think I'm going to have a whisk."

The groom broom says, "How can that be possible? We haven't even swept together!"

✱ A FUNERAL SERVICE IS HELD for a woman. As the pallbearers carry the casket out, they accidentally bump into a wall. They hear a faint moan. They open the casket and find that the woman is actually alive. She lives for ten more years and then dies. They have another funeral for her. At the end of the service, the pallbearers carry out the casket. As they are walking, the husband cries out, "Watch out for the wall!"

✱ A BUS FULL OF HOUSEWIVES going on a picnic crashes with no survivors. Each husband cries for a week, but one husband continues for more than two weeks. When asked why, he replies miserably, "My wife missed the bus."

✱ TWO FRIENDS ARE FISHING ON a lake. "I read in a book the other day that on the average day, a man speaks over 35,000 words and a woman speaks slightly over 30,000."

The second man answers, "That sounds about right, but my wife usually waits to say her 30,000 words after I get home from work."

Weddings

✱ LAST WEEK, I WENT TO an incredibly emotional wedding. The bride was crying. The groom was broken up. Even the wedding cake was in tiers.

✱ ON THEIR FIRST NIGHT TOGETHER, a newlywed couple go to change clothes. The new bride comes out of the bathroom showered and wearing a beautiful robe. The proud husband says, "My dear, we are married now, you can open your robe." The beautiful young woman opens her robe, and he is astonished. "Oh, oh, aaaahhh," he exclaims. "My God, you are so beautiful, let me take your picture."

Puzzled she asks, "My picture?"

He answers, "Yes, my dear, so I can carry your beauty next to my heart forever." She smiles and he takes her picture, and then he heads into the bathroom to shower. He comes out wearing his robe and the new wife asks, "Why do you wear a robe? We are married now."

At that the man opens his robe and she exclaims, "Oh, oh my! Let me get a picture."

He beams and asks why and she answers, "So I can get it enlarged!"

✱ A FIGHT BROKE OUT AT a wedding. The first officer on scene asked what happened. Tommy stepped forward and said, "I am the best man and I was dancing with the bride. Then, out of nowhere, the groom storms over and kicks her right in the fanny." "That must have hurt," said the officer. "Heck yeah, it did!" replied Tommy. "He broke three of my fingers!"

✱ A LITTLE BOY AT A wedding asks his mom, "Mommy, why do brides wear white dresses at their wedding?"

The mom responds, "Because it's the happiest day of her life."

The kid responds, "Then how come the groom wears black?"

Divorce

✱ WHY DID FROSTY THE SNOWMAN want a divorce? He thought his wife was a flake.

✱ A MAN GOES INTO A jewelry store on his lunch hour to buy his mistress a necklace. After looking at a few, he decides on a very expensive diamond pendant.

"Is this for your wife?" the clerk asks as she wraps it in the finest paper. The man turns to see his wife entering the store, out on her daily errands, and replies to the clerk, "It is now."

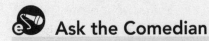 **Ask the Comedian**

✳ A MAN GOES AWAY ON business. He e-mails his wife from the road and says he'll be home that night because the trip wrapped up earlier than expected. When he gets home, he walks into the bedroom to find his wife in bed with another man. Without a word, the husband leaves the room and goes down to the local bar. He explains the whole situation to the bartender.

"Well, why don't you call her and talk to her. Maybe there is an explanation for all of this."

The man picks up his cell phone and calls his house. His wife answers and before she can say a word he yells, "Why did I come home to find you in bed with another man?" The wife calmly responds, "Because I just got around to checking my e-mail."

✳ A WIFE COMES DOWNSTAIRS BEFORE a dinner date with her husband.

"Do I look fat in this dress?" the wife asks.

"Do I look dumb in this shirt?" the husband replies.

✳ A WIFE STOPS BY THE office to visit her husband. He's been working incredibly hard, often staying late hours to finish a big deal. The wife walks into his office to find his secretary sitting on his lap. The husband spots her and wastes no time, saying to his secretary, ". . . and in conclusion, ladies and gentlemen of the board, budget cuts or no budget cuts, I cannot continue to operate this office efficiently with just one chair."

✳ A MAN PULLS INTO A driveway and sees a naked man running past his house. The man calls out, "Why are you jogging naked?"

The naked runner says, "Because you came home from work early!"

✳ WHAT DO YOU CALL A man who has lost 90 percent of his intelligence? Divorced.

✳ A WOMAN WALKS INTO A pet store and sees a handsome bright red parrot. She asks the cashier how much the parrot is. The cashier says, "I'll sell it, but I should warn you, it was donated by a brothel, so it might have picked up some colorful language."

The woman says, "Oh, that's okay." She buys the parrot and takes it home.

When she takes the towel off its cage, the parrot looks at her and says, "Awk. New madam. Hello madam."

A few hours later, the woman's two teenage daughters come home from school. The parrot looks at them and says, "Awk. New girls. Hello girls."

A couple hours after that, the woman's husband Phil comes home from work. The parrot looks at him and says, "Awk. Hi Phil."

✳ A WOMAN FILES FOR DIVORCE from her husband on the grounds of mental cruelty. She claims that his treatment of her was so severe it caused her to lose 30 pounds in just a few months. "Divorce granted," the judge says after hearing the entire case.

"Not yet!" the woman pleads. "I'm still ten pounds away from my goal!"

✳ BETTY AND TIM DIE IN a car accident the night before their wedding. In heaven, they ask St. Peter if they can still be married. "Well, let me find out if this is possible. Stay here and I will be right back."

Six months pass and St. Peter returns. "Yes, we can do this for you."

The couple says, "Well, as we have spent so much time together waiting for your answer, we need to know—if things don't work out, is there a possibility that we can get divorced?"

St. Peter answers, "It took me six months to find a priest up here—how long do you think it will take me to find a lawyer?"

✳ WHAT DO A TORNADO AND a redneck divorce have in common? In the end, someone is going to lose a trailer.

Famous Funnies

"I don't have a girlfriend. But I do know a woman who'd be mad at me for saying that."—Mitch Hedberg

✳ IF MARRIAGE IS GRAND, WHAT is divorce? Ten grand.

✳ A MAN RUSHES INTO HIS house and yells to his wife, "Honey, pack up your things! I just won the lottery!"

She replies excitedly, "Oh my god! Okay! Should I pack for warm weather or cold weather?"

The husband responds, "I don't care. Just as long as you're out of the house by lunch!"

✳ AFTER BEING MARRIED FOR THIRTY years, a man takes a look at his wife and says, "Honey, do you realize that thirty years ago, I had a cheap apartment, a cheap car, slept on a pull-out bed, and watched a 13-inch black-and-white TV, but I got to sleep every night with a hot twenty-one-year-old blonde? Now, we have a nice house, nice car, big bed, and plasma screen TV, but I'm sleeping with a fifty-one-year-old blonde. It seems to me that you are not holding up your side of things."

The wife, a very reasonable woman, tells him: "Go out and find a hot twenty-one-year-old blonde, and I'll make sure that you're once again living in a cheap apartment, driving a cheap car, sleeping on a sofa bed, and if you're lucky, you'll have a small television to watch."

✳ A WOMAN VISITS A FORTUNETELLER who tells her, "Prepare yourself to be a widow. Your husband will die a violent and horrible death this year." Visibly shaken, the woman takes a few deep breaths, steadies her voice, and asks, "Will I be acquitted?"

✳ HAVE YOU HEARD OF THE new divorced Barbie doll? She comes with all of Ken's stuff.

✳ A WOMAN WAKES DURING THE night to find that her husband is not in bed. She puts on her robe and goes downstairs. He is sitting at the kitchen table with a cup of coffee in front of him. He appears to be in deep thought, just staring at the wall. She sees him wipe a tear from his eye and take a sip of his coffee.

"What's the matter, dear? Why are you down here at this time of night?" she asks.

"Do you remember twenty years ago when we were dating and you were only sixteen?" he asks.

"Yes, I do," she replies.

"Do you remember when your father caught us in the back seat of my car making out?"

"Yes, I remember."

"Do you remember when he shoved that shotgun in my face and said, 'Either you marry my daughter or spend twenty years in jail'?"

"Yes, I do," she says.

He wipes another tear from his cheek and says, "You know . . . I would have gotten out today."

CHAPTER 4

Occasions and Holidays

Holidays are a time to be happy and to enjoy the company of loved ones. What better way to spread cheer and good will than with a small arsenal of jokes perfect for the Christmas cocktail party or over a pint on St. Paddy's Day? These jokes about the holidays are sure to make even the biggest Grinch laugh like jolly old St. Nick.

Christmas/Hanukkah

❋ THE WORST THING ABOUT OFFICE holiday parties is having to spend the entire day after looking for a new job.

❋ DID YOU HEAR ABOUT THE Advent calendar that passed away? Its days were numbered.

❋ IT WAS CHRISTMAS TIME, AND the judge was feeling a little benevolent and filled with holiday spirit. "What exactly is the charge?" he asked counsel.

"The man standing before you is charged with doing his Christmas shopping early."

"Shopping early?" the judge replied. "Well, what's wrong with that?"

The prosecutor replied, "He was doing his shopping before the stores were open."

Famous Funnies

"The one thing women don't want to find in their stockings on Christmas morning is their husband."—Joan Rivers

✳ A MAN HANDS HIS GIRLFRIEND a small package on Christmas morning, the size of a jewelry box. The woman gets incredibly excited and rips the package open to find a deck of playing cards.

"What the heck is this?" she yells and throws the deck of cards into the man's lap. "What?" the man responds. "You said all you wanted for Christmas was something with diamonds in it!"

✳ WHAT DO YOU CALL AN elf that lives in Beverly Hills? Welfy.

✳ DURING THE RUSH OF THE holiday season, Sarah completely forgot to mail a Christmas card to her best friend. She hurries into the post office with a card and asks the postal service worker for a first-class stamp.

"Do I have to put this stamp on myself?" she asks.

"No," the postal employee replies. "You can put it right on the envelope."

✳ WHY DO DOGS LOVE CHRISTMAS? It's the only time of the year that the bathroom is indoors.

✳ A GUY BOUGHT HIS WIFE a beautiful diamond ring for Hanukkah. After hearing about this extravagant gift, a friend of his says, "I thought she wanted one of those sporty four-wheel-drive vehicles."

"She did," he replies. "But where was I going to find a fake Jeep?"

✱ A COUPLE ARE CHRISTMAS SHOPPING. The shopping center is packed, and as the wife walks through one of the stores, she is surprised when she looks around to find that her husband is nowhere to be seen. She is quite upset because they had a lot to do. She becomes so worried that she calls him to ask where he is. In a quiet voice he says, "Do you remember the jeweler's we went into about five years ago where you fell in love with that diamond necklace that we couldn't afford, and I told you that I would get it for you one day?"

The wife gets choked up and starts to cry and says, "Yes, I do remember that shop."

He replies, "Well, I'm in the pub next door."

 Comedy Facts

Musicians and *Saturday Night Live* have a rich history, but no other musical act was more important to SNL creator Lorne Michaels than The Beatles. In one famous sketch, Michaels appeared on camera to offer the Fab Four $3,000 to appear on the show. Michaels would find out years later that John Lennon and Paul McCartney were watching the show that evening and considered hopping into a cab and showing up at the show but were "too tired" to make the trip.

✱ A MALL SANTA IS TAKEN aback when a woman, around the age of thirty, gets in line to sit on his lap. When it is her turn, she sits down, and Santa tells her, "We don't normally listen to the Christmas wishes of adults."

"I've only got one wish," the woman says, "and it's for my mother."

"Oh, that's nice of you," the mall Santa says. "Okay, we'll make an exception this time. What would you like me to bring your mother for Christmas this year?"

The woman answers, "A son-in-law."

✳ THERE ARE FOUR STAGES OF life that involve Santa Claus—first you believe in Santa Claus, then you stop believing in Santa Claus, then you become Santa Claus to your family, and then you look like Santa Claus.

Comedy Facts

The founders of modern American stand-up comedy include Jack Benny, Bob Hope, George Burns, Fred Allen, and Milton Berle. All of these performers came from vaudeville. Other popular comedic training grounds were from the "Borscht Belt," which referred to a group of venues (primarily in the Catskill Mountains of New York state) that were popular spots for Jewish performers of the time and the chitlin' circuit. The chitlin' circuit was a term used to describe the clubs around the country where it was acceptable for African Americans to perform. Popular comedians who got their start in the chitlin' circuit include Redd Foxx, Richard Pryor, Jimmie Walker, and Moms Mabley.

✳ WHAT IS THE MOST POPULAR Christmas wine? "This isn't what I asked for!"

✳ A GUY DECIDES TO BUY his son a dog for Christmas. On the way home from work, he sees a sign in front of a house in his neighborhood that reads, "Talking Dog for Sale." He rings the bell and the owner tells him the dog is in the backyard. The guy goes into the backyard and sees a black mutt just sitting there.

"You talk?" he asks.

"Sure do," the dog replies.

"So, what's your story?"

The dog looks up and says, "Well, I discovered my gift of talking pretty young and I wanted to help the government, so I told the CIA about my gift, and in no time they had me jetting from country to country, sitting in rooms with spies and world leaders, because no one figured a dog would be eavesdropping. I was one of their most valuable spies eight years running. The jetting around really tired me out, and I knew I wasn't getting any younger and I wanted to settle down. So I signed up for a job at the airport to do some undercover security work, mostly wandering near suspicious characters and listening in. I uncovered some incredible dealings there and was awarded a batch of medals. Had a wife, a mess of puppies, and now I'm just retired."

The guy is amazed. He goes back in and asks the owner what he wants for the dog.

The owner says, "Ten dollars."

The guy says, "This dog is amazing. Why on earth are you selling him so cheap?"

"'Cause he's a liar."

* WHAT DO YOU CALL A kid who doesn't believe in Santa? A rebel without a Claus.

* WHY IS CHRISTMAS JUST LIKE a day at work? You do all the work and the fat guy with the suit gets all the credit.

* WHY WAS SANTA'S LITTLE HELPER depressed? Because the poor fella had low elf esteem.

 Ask the Comedian

What happens if people don't laugh at a joke?
There could be numerous reasons why people don't laugh at a joke. Perhaps they just don't find the joke or topic particularly funny. They might have heard the joke before or aren't really in much of a mood to laugh. Being unable to elicit a laugh isn't always your fault. The two most effective ways to recover from a joke missing its mark are to either accept the few uncomfortable moments and continue the conversation or do what legendary funny man Johnny Carson did when a joke bombed—make a joke about the joke bombing.

✳ WHAT DO YOU GET WHEN you cross a snowman with a vampire? Frostbite.

✳ ON CHRISTMAS MORNING A WOMAN tells her husband, "I just dreamed that you gave me a beautiful diamond necklace. What do you think it means?"

"You'll know tonight," he says. That evening just before opening presents, the husband comes home with a small package and gives it to his wife. Delighted, she opens it only to find a book titled *The Meaning of Dreams*.

✳ ADMIRING THE CHRISTMAS TREES DISPLAYED in his neighbors' windows, a child asks his father, "Daddy, can we have a Hanukkah tree?"

"What? No, of course not," says his father.

"Why not?" asks the child again.

Bewildered, his father replies, "Because the last time we had dealings with a lighted bush we spent forty years wandering the desert."

✳ THE MALL SANTA HAD MANY children asking for electric trains. "If you get a train," he tells each one, "you know your dad is going to want to play with it too. Is that okay?" After he asks that question of little Tommy, the boy becomes very quiet. Trying to move the conversation along, Santa asks what else he would like Santa to bring him. The boy promptly replies, "Another train."

✳ ON THE FIRST DAY OF Hanukkah, a grandmother is giving her grandson directions to her apartment. He is coming to visit with his new wife.

"You come to the front door of the condominium complex. I am in apartment 2B. There is a big panel at the front door. With your elbow, push button 2B. I'll buzz you in. Come inside and the elevator is on the right. Hit the up button with your elbow, get in, and with your other elbow hit the number two. When you exit the elevator, I'm the second door on the right. Ring my doorbell with your elbow and I'll let you in."

"Grandma, that sounds easy," replies the grandson. "But why am I hitting all these buttons with my elbow?"

His grandmother answers, "You're coming to visit empty-handed?"

✳ A WOMAN GOES TO THE post office for stamps for Hanukkah cards. She asks the cashier for stamps and the cashier replies, "What denomination?" The woman thinks for a moment and responds, "I'll take six Orthodox, twelve Conservative, and thirty-two Reform, please."

 Famous Funnies

"That's the true spirit of Christmas; people being helped by people other than me."—Jerry Seinfeld

✳ A SON IS VISITING HIS mother the week after Hanukkah wearing one of the two sweaters she'd given him as a gift for the holiday. As he walks into her house, instead of saying hello, the mother says, "What's wrong? You didn't like the other sweater I got you?"

Valentine's Day

✳ A MAN WANTS VALENTINE'S DAY to be special, so he buys a bottle of absinthe and stops by the florist's to order a bouquet of his wife's favorite flower: white anemones. Unfortunately, the florist is sold out of flowers and has only a few stems of feathery ferns. The man asks the florist to make a bouquet out of the ferns and the flask of liquor. He adds a card and proceeds home. After a romantic candlelight dinner, he presents his wife with the gift. She opens the card to read, "Absinthe makes the heart grow fonder."

With a tear in her eye, she whispers to him lovingly, "Yes, and with fronds like these, who needs anemones?"

✻ TWO ANTENNAE MET ON A roof on Valentine's Day. They fell in love and got married. Their wedding ceremony wasn't anything fancy, but the reception was awesome.

✻ WHAT DO FARMERS GIVE THEIR wives on Valentine's Day? Hogs and kisses.

✻ WHAT IS THE DIFFERENCE BETWEEN a calendar and you? A calendar has a date on Valentine's Day.

 ## Comedy Facts

In 1972, George Carlin released an album of stand-up comedy titled *Class Clown*. A track on the album titled "Seven Words You Can Never Say on Television" was a monologue in which Carlin identified these "dirty" words and discussed how these particular words could not be used on television or radio, regardless of the context. That same year, Carlin was arrested for disturbing the peace for performing the routine, and saying the words, at a show in Milwaukee.

✻ WHAT DID THE FRENCH CHEF give his wife for Valentine's Day? A hug and a quiche.

✻ DID YOU KNOW VALENTINE'S DAY is a huge holiday for skunks? They are all very scent-imental.

✻ A YOUNG MAN IS WAITING in line at a post office when he notices an older man in the corner of the office, licking stamps that say *Love* on them and putting them on bright pink envelopes. The man then takes a bottle of perfume from his jacket pocket and sprays the envelopes. Curiosity gets the better of the young man, so he walks over and asks the older man what he is doing. "I'm sending out five hundred Valentine's cards with the phrase 'Guess Who?' written inside."

"Why?" the young man asks.

The man smiles and says, "Because I'm a divorce lawyer."

St. Patrick's Day

❋ WHY DO LEPRECHAUNS MAKE GREAT secretaries? They've got great shorthand.

 Joke Essentials

Put the funny word at the end. If there's a funny-sounding word within the punch line of your joke, try to arrange the sentence so that the funny word falls at the end of the joke. Words with hard sounds are usually the funniest.

❋ A PRIEST IS DRIVING HOME from the bar on St. Patrick's Day. He mistakenly takes an empty bottle of wine with him and tosses it onto the floor on the passenger side of the car. He's pulled over by a cop, who smells alcohol on the priest's breath and spots the empty wine bottle on the floor of the car. The cop asks the priest, "Father, have you been drinking tonight?"

"No sir, nothing but water," says the priest.

The trooper says, "Then why do I smell wine?"

The priest thinks for a moment and exclaims, "Good Lord! He's done it again!"

❋ WHAT TYPE OF LAWN FURNITURE is only used on St. Patrick's Day? Paddy O'Furniture.

The parishioner replies, "I'm already in the Army of the Lord, pastor."

The pastor questions, "Then how come I don't see you in church except at Christmas and Easter?"

The parishioner whispers, "I'm in the secret service."

✱ A YOUNG BOY IS SITTING in his grandmother's kitchen, watching her prepare Thanksgiving dinner. "What are you doing to the turkey?" the boy asks his grandmother. "Oh, I'm just stuffing the bird," his grandmother replies. "Wow, that's cool," the boy remarks. "Are you going to hang it in the living room next to the deer head?"

✱ A WOMAN IS LOOKING FOR a Thanksgiving turkey, but can't find a bird big enough to feed her massive family. She asks the stock boy, "Do these turkeys get any bigger?" The stock boy replies, "No, they've stopped growing, ma'am. Those turkeys are dead."

Halloween and New Year's Eve

✱ WHAT SHOULD YOU DO THE moment you realize your house is surrounded by zombies? Pray that it's Halloween.

✱ WHY WAS THE STUDENT VAMPIRE tired in the morning? Because he was up all night studying for his blood test!

✱ HOW DID THE GHOST SAY goodbye to the vampire? "So long sucker!"

✱ WHY DO GHOSTS LOVE GOING out to bars? Strictly for the booooooos.

✱ A NEW YEAR'S RESOLUTION IS something that goes in one year and out the other.

✱ WHAT'S THE PROBLEM WITH JOGGING on New Year's Eve? The ice falls out of your drink!

✱ WHAT DO YOU CALL ALWAYS having a date for New Year's Eve? Social security.

✱ AT A NEW YEAR'S EVE party, a woman stands up on the bar and announces that it is almost midnight. She says that at midnight, she wants every husband to stand next to the one person who makes his life worth living. As the clock strikes twelve, the bartender is almost crushed to death.

Comedy Facts

The first comedy album was released in 1958 on the Verve Records label. It was the first long-play comedy album. The title of the album was *The Future Lies Ahead* and the comedian, Mort Sahl, is considered the first modern stand-up comic.

✱ AT A NEW YEAR'S EVE party, a man turns to his friend and asks for a smoke. "I thought you made a New Year's resolution to give up smoking," his friend says.

"I'm in the process of quitting," the man replies. "I am in the middle of phase one." "Phase one?" his friend replies.

"Yes." The man laughs, grabbing the cigarette. "Starting today I've quit buying."

CHAPTER 5

Work and Occupations

I t's unfortunate that many people spend more time at work and with coworkers than with their own family, but that's just the way this world works. Since you spend the bulk of the day surrounded by near strangers, why not share these gags about jobs, offices, and bosses? They are sure to have all the office drones grinning in their cubicles.

Office Jokes

❋ A COWORKER IS SHOWING THE latest company hire around the office. "How long have you worked here?" the new hire asks.

"Ever since they threatened to fire me," the coworker answers.

❋ NO MATTER HOW OFTEN YOU push the envelope, it will always remain stationery.

❋ "YOUR COUGH SOUNDS MUCH BETTER today," a man said to his coworker in the next cubicle.

"Yeah," said the sick man, "I was up all night practicing it."

❋ A MAN SHOWS UP FOR work with his arm in a cast.

"What happened to you?" his assistant asks.

"I broke my arm in two places yesterday."

"Man, that sucks," says his assistant. "It would probably be a good idea to avoid those two places from now on."

✱ A MAN IS BEGGING A judge to let him off jury duty because of his job. "I'm sure your company can get along fine without you for a few days," the judge tells the man.

"I know," the man answers. "But that's what I'm trying to prevent them from figuring out."

✱ A MAN GOES ON A job interview. The interviewer tells him that they are looking to hire someone who is responsible. "Well, I'm your man," the applicant replies. "At my last job, whenever anything went wrong, they said I was responsible."

✱ "BILL," A SAD-FACED MAN SAYS to his coworker, "I just heard the news about your uncle falling off that cliff. I'm terribly sorry. Were the two of you close?"

"We were just close enough for me to push him," Bill replies.

✱ AN OFFICE MANAGER IS INTERVIEWING an applicant. He asks the woman if she has any unusual talents. She says she'd actually won a few national crossword puzzle contests. "Sounds good," the office manager replies, "but we want someone who will be just as intelligent during office hours."

"Oh," says the applicant. "That's good because that's when I do most of my puzzles."

✱ A FEW MINUTES INTO THE monthly speech from the owner of the company, the microphone cuts out. He decides to keep going with the speech, and project his voice through the room. Halfway through his talk, he stops and asks, "Can you all hear me?"

"I can," a man says in the front row, "but I wouldn't mind switching seats with someone in the back who can't."

✱ A WIFE ASKS HER HUSBAND how his day at work went. "It was awful," the man explains, pouring himself a stiff drink. "All of our computer systems shut down today so we had to do everything manually."

"That sounds awful," the wife consoles.

"You're telling me," he replies after a sip. "I had to keep shuffling the deck of cards for solitaire by hand."

 Comedy Facts

Already a legend in vaudeville and in stage performances around the country, Frank Fay became hugely popular as the "master of ceremonies" at New York's Palace Theatre. Fay is credited with creating the style of performing recognized today as stand-up. These performers spoke directly to the audience as themselves and not in character.

✳ THE HEAD OF HUMAN RESOURCES is interviewing a potential candidate for the open position of corporate attorney. "Would you consider yourself an honest lawyer?" the HR person asks in the interview.

"Honest?" the lawyer responds. "Let me tell you how honest I am. My father sold everything he had to put me through law school. After my very first case, I paid him back in full."

"That's very impressive," the HR person admits. "What was the case?"

The attorney fidgets in his seat and says, "He sued me for the money."

✳ WHAT'S FORREST GUMP'S E-MAIL PASSWORD at work? 1forrest1

✳ REACHING THE END OF A job interview, the human resources officer asks a young engineer fresh out of MIT, "What type of starting salary are you looking for?"

The engineer replies, "In the region of $150,000 a year, depending on the benefits package."

The interviewer asks, "Well, what would you say to a package of six weeks' vacation, fourteen paid holidays, full medical and dental benefits, the company matches retirement fund to 50 percent of salary, and a new company car every two years?"

The engineer sits up straight and says, "Wow! Are you kidding?" The interviewer replies, "Yes, but you started it."

✳ A BRAND-NEW AD FIRM PUTS a job posting online for a "Problem Solver" and lists the salary at $100,000 per year. Ted applies for the gig, gets an interview, and is offered the job. "That's amazing," Ted says to the hiring manager. "But this is a brand-new firm. How can you afford to pay me such a high salary?"

"Well," the manager replies, "that's your first problem to solve."

✳ A BOSS SHOWS HIS EMPLOYEE his new sports car. "That is amazing," the employee responds.

"Isn't it?" replies the boss. "And if you set your goals higher and work even harder this year, I can get an even better car next year."

✳ THE HUMAN RESOURCES MANAGER IS interviewing a potential candidate for an incredibly important position within the company. During the interview, the manager takes another glance at the candidate's resume and realizes he'd been fired from every job he ever held.

"You've been fired from every single job you've ever held. How on earth does this make you a strong candidate for this position?" the HR manager asks.

"Well," answered the man, "if my resume shows one thing, it's that I'm not a quitter."

✳ DON STARTS HIS OWN CONSULTING firm and leases a brand-new office. On his first day, a stranger walks into the office. Trying to look important for a potential client, Don picks up the phone and begins to discuss a really huge deal he's working on. He talks for another few minutes, seals the deal, and hangs up the phone. "Sorry about that. What can I help you with?" Don asks the stranger. "I'm here to hook up the phones," the man replies.

✳ WITH THE COMPANY LOSING MONEY, the CEO sends out an e-mail to the entire staff with the subject line CASH BONUS FOR

BEST IDEA. The CEO explains that anyone on staff who can come up with an idea to save the company money will win a $200 bonus. A woman in the accounting department wins the prize. Her idea was to reduce future prize bonuses to just ten dollars.

✳ A BOSS CATCHES AN EMPLOYEE walking in the door at 10 A.M. The boss is angry and barks at the employee, "You should have been here at 8 A.M.!"

"Why?" the employee asks. "What happened at eight?"

✳ A SECRETARY WALKS INTO HER boss's office and tells him, "I've got some really bad news for you, sir."

The boss asks, "Why do you always have to give me bad news? How about some good news for a change?"

"Fine," she replies. "The good news is you're not too old to have another kid."

✳ A MAN RETURNS HOME FROM work and breaks the bad news to his wife. "I got fired today," the man says. "My boss said it was due in large part to my awful communication skills."

"What did you say when he told you that?" his wife asks.

The unemployed man answers, "I didn't know what to say."

 Comedy Facts

In 2013, comedian David Scott broke the Guinness World Record for longest stand-up comedian performance. The previous record was forty hours. Scott performed for forty hours and eight minutes. The rules stated the comedian couldn't repeat the same joke in a four-hour span, could only take a five-minute break every hour, had to stand on a designated spot on stage, and the audience had to contain at least ten people at all times.

✳ A BOSS CALLS A NEW intern into his office. "You definitely march to the beat of a different drummer," the boss tells the intern.

"Is that good?" the intern asks.

"Well it could be," the boss explains, "if your drummer didn't bang so darn slowly."

✳ "THIS BRAND-NEW LAPTOP WILL DO half your job for you," the IT guy explains to the senior vice president of the company.

"Perfect," the vice president replies. "Can I get two then?"

✳ LAST WEEK, A COMPUTER PROGRAMMER drowned at sea. The beach was packed with people, and he yelled out "F1! F1!" in distress, but no one understood.

The Arts

✳ A WORLD-FAMOUS AUTHOR WAS HAVING lunch with his editor. "I don't know," he said, "I feel like my early work is much better than the stuff I'm putting out now."

"That's nonsense," the editor said. "Your writing is the same now as it was back then. It's your taste that's gotten better."

✳ AN ACTOR IS GIVING AN awful performance of Macbeth. His work is so awful the crowd begins to boo in the middle of his monologue. The actor stops mid-sentence and yells out to the crowd, "Don't boo me! I didn't write this garbage."

✳ WHY WAS THE LIMBO DANCER shocked when his wallet was stolen right out of his back pocket? Because he didn't think anyone could stoop so low.

✳ A STRUGGLING ARTIST STOPS BY the studio where his recent work is hanging for sale. The owner tells him he has good news and bad news.

"The good news is that a man dropped by the studio today and put in an offer to buy every single piece. He just wanted my guarantee that the works would be worth twice what he paid if you were to pass away. I told him they would double, possibly triple in value. So he bought them all."

"Whoa!" exclaims the artist. "That's fantastic. What could be the bad news?"

"The guy is your doctor," the owner says.

Restaurants and Bars

✳ A WAITER RETURNS TO THE table to ask the customer how his meal is so far. "How did you find your steak?" the waiter asks.

"I just pushed a ton of mashed potatoes to the side and there it was," says the man.

✳ ON THE LAST MISSION TO the moon, NASA set up a restaurant. It didn't last very long. The food was good, but there was no atmosphere.

✳ A MAN IS STANDING ON a busy street corner with a placard over his chest for the local McDonald's. On the front, in big bold letters, are the words *Free Big Mac*. A homeless man stumbles over and asks the man, "What is Mac serving time for?"

✳ WHAT DID THE ZEN BUDDHIST say to the hotdog vendor? Make me one with everything.

✳ A BARTENDER ANSWERS THE PHONE, and the man on the other end asks if they serve women at the bar. "Nope," the bartender replies, "you've got to bring your own."

✳ A DUMB GUY CALLS TO yell at the pizza man at his local shop. "I got this pizza delivered and I specifically asked to have the pie cut into six slices. This pie is cut in eight slices!"

"What's the big deal?" the pizza man wonders.

"There is no way I'll be able to eat all these!" the man yells.

✳ A POPULAR WAITER PASSED AWAY suddenly. Not having had a chance to say goodbye, a group of his best customers hired a medium to speak with him in the afterlife. The medium gathered the group around a table and began to call the waiter's name. "Bruce Mallory!" the medium called out. "Bruce! Bruce Mallory!" the medium yelled into the air again. Still nothing. The medium called for a third time and suddenly a figure appeared in the air. It was the spirit of Bruce Mallory. "Bruce, it's your favorite customers," one man said to the spirit. "Why didn't you come the first time we called you?"

"Because," Bruce said from beyond, "this isn't my table."

✳ A WOMAN IS HAVING LUNCH at a restaurant with an open kitchen. She orders a burger and notices that the chef takes a giant chunk of meat, puts it under his armpit to roll it into a ball, slams it down on the grill, and starts to make her burger. "That's the grossest thing I've ever seen!" the woman says to the waitress.

"That's nothing," the waitress replies, "you should see him make doughnuts in the morning."

✳ A WAITRESS IN A DINER brings a man the soup du jour, but the man is a bit dismayed. "Good heavens," he says, "what is this?" "Why, it's bean soup," she replies. "I don't care what it's been," he replies. "What is it now?"

✳ A MAN SITS DOWN FOR dinner and asks his waiter, "How do you prepare the chicken?" The waiter replies, "We don't, the chef just chops off his head when his back is turned."

✳ TWO WOMEN VISIT THEIR FAVORITE lunch spot after a day of shopping. While ordering, the first woman makes a specific request of the waiter. "Can you please make sure my water glass is clean? We were here for lunch last week and my water glass was filthy." A few minutes later the waiter returns to the table with their lunch and drink order.

"Okay, which one of you ladies ordered the clean glass?"

✳ A CUSTOMER ASKS TO SEE the manager of the restaurant where he's eating dinner. "This place is filthy," the man says to the manager.

"That's outrageous!" exclaims the manager. "You could eat your dinner off our dining room floor!"

"That's my issue," says the customer. "It looks like someone already has."

✳ A MAN SITS DOWN AT the counter of a diner and orders breakfast.

"How do you want your eggs cooked?" the waiter asks.

"Does it affect the price?" the man asks. The waiter says it makes no difference.

"Okay," says the man, "then I'll have them cooked with potatoes and sausage."

Sales

✳ A SALESMAN IS PEDDLING HIS goods from door to door in a massive high-rise building. He knocks at a young man's apartment and asks him, "Would you like to buy a top-of-the-line toothbrush? It's only ten dollars."

"Ten bucks for a toothbrush!" the man yells. "What moron would pay ten dollars for a toothbrush? You're out of your mind."

"All right then," the salesman continues, "then how about a fresh-baked brownie for a dollar?" The man thinks it over and says, "Okay, why not?"

The salesman hands over the brownie. The man takes a bite and spits it out onto the floor in the hallway.

"My god, that tastes like crap!" he yells.

"Well, that's because it is crap," the salesman explains. "So can I interest you in a toothbrush?"

✳ A TRAVELING SALESMAN IS TRAPPED at a hotel in Denver because of a massive snowstorm. He e-mails the home office in

New York to say that he'll be delayed a few days. His boss e-mails back, "Start your vacation immediately."

✳ THREE INSURANCE SALESMEN ARE HAVING drinks and boasting about each company's service. The first one says, "When one of our insured died suddenly on Monday, we got the news that evening and were able to process the claim for the wife and mailed a check on Wednesday evening."

The second one says, "When one of our insured died without warning on Monday, we learned of it in two hours and were able to hand-deliver a check the same evening."

The last salesman says, "That's nothing. Our office is on the twentieth floor in the Sears Tower. One of our insured, who was washing a window on the eighty-fifth floor, slipped and fell. We handed him his check as he passed our floor."

 Ask the Comedian

What happens if my joke angers someone?
Unless the joke pokes fun at a specific ethnicity or stereotype, it's very rare that a written joke will anger a person. Making fun of a person or joking at another person's expense could make someone angry. If either of these is the case, it's best to just apologize for offending the person.

✳ A BUSINESSMAN IS IN A VIP lounge awaiting a flight when he notices Donald Trump just a few seats away. The man walks up to Trump and introduces himself and asks a favor. "I'm expecting a prospective client in a few minutes. It would help me seal the deal if you passed by while we were talking and said hello. It would really impress him and the deal would be mine."

Trump agrees. A few minutes later the man is talking to his client. The plane begins to board and Trump, true to his word, walks by the two men and says, "Hey, pal, how's business?"

The man looks up and responds, "Beat it, Trump, I'm in the middle of a meeting."

Health and Medicine

✳ A DENTIST IS EXAMINING A woman's teeth. Her teeth are perfect, but before the exam is over, he makes an odd request. "Would you do me a favor?" the dentist asks. "I'm going to turn this drill on. When I do, I need you to scream as loud as possible."

The woman is shocked. "Why would you want me to do that? You've got a waiting room full of patients."

"Exactly," replies the dentist, "and I've also got tickets for the game in a half hour."

✳ WHAT DID THE ACUPUNCTURE TEACHER say to his prize student? "You were born for this jab."

✳ A NURSE BURSTS INTO THE doctor's office with awful news. "Dr. Johnson!" she yells. "They just found Mr. Bay dead in the hallway. Didn't you just give him a clean bill of health and send him on his way?"

"My god, I did!" the doctor yells. "Quick, let's retrieve the body and make it look like he was just walking in!"

✳ WHY DID THE DERMATOLOGIST FIND it so hard to keep his customers happy? He was always making rash decisions.

 Famous Funnies

"Children are smarter than any of us. Know how I know that? I don't know one child with a full-time job and children."—Bill Hicks

✳ DID YOU HEAR ABOUT THE psychologist who went back to school to be a proctologist? He spends all day dealing with odds and ends.

✳ TWO PSYCHOLOGISTS RUN INTO EACH other at their twentieth college reunion. One of the men looks like he just graduated from school while the other looks old, tired, and run down from life. The older-looking psychologist asks the other, "What's your secret for looking so young? Listening to other people's problems every day, all day long, for years and years, has made an old man of me."

The younger-looking psychologist replies, "Who listens?"

✳ THE DEFENSE TEAM IS CROSS-EXAMINING a star witness in a murder case. He is the young doctor who performed the autopsy on the deceased. Trying to ruin his credibility, the lead defense attorney asks, "What makes you such an authority on this, sir? Just how many autopsies have you performed on dead people in your young career?" The doctor thinks for a moment and replies, "Well, all of my autopsies have been performed on dead people."

✳ A PSYCHIATRIST IS COMMENDING A mental patient on the tremendous progress he's made over the last few months. "When you first stepped in my office, you thought you were the King of England. Now you realize you're just a man like anyone else. How does that make you feel?"

"I feel so depressed," the man answers.

"Depressed? Why?" the psychiatrist asks.

"Well, I used to be a somebody, but now I'm a nobody!"

✳ DID YOU HEAR ABOUT THE woman who was robbed by an unemployed acupuncturist? She was stabbed more than 167 times but she felt awesome the next day.

✳ WHY DID THE MASSEUSE HAVE to close up his shop? He kept rubbing people the wrong way.

✳ WHAT DO YOU CALL A stork that only delivers un-intelligent babies? A dope peddler.

Retail

✳ "I'LL TAKE SOME PORK CHOPS," the woman tells the butcher, "and make them lean."

"No problem," the butcher replies. "Which way?"

✳ A MUSIC STORE WAS ROBBED last week. The robbers made off with the lute.

✳ A YOUNG MAN WALKS INTO a record store and asks the clerk, "Do you have anything by The Doors?"

"Sure," replies the clerk, "a mop bucket and a fire extinguisher."

✳ A MAN GOES BACK TO a bookstore to complain about a recent purchase. "I bought this book last week called *The Biggest Cowards in History*, but the minute I opened the book, all of the pages fell out." The sales clerk looks at the book and explains, "Well that's because it's got no spine."

✳ A STORE MANAGER WATCHES FROM a distance as a salesperson argues with a customer. After a few minutes, the customer storms out of the store.

"I saw what just happened," the manager says, "and I guess you've forgotten my motto of 'the customer is always right.'"

"I know," the salesperson says, "but . . ."

"No buts," says the manager. "The customer is always right."

"Fine," responds the salesperson.

"What were you two arguing about?" the manager asks.

The salesperson answers, "He called you an idiot."

✳ A MAN WALKS INTO A pet store, interested in a parrot. He notices a gorgeous bird with a red ribbon on its right ankle and a blue ribbon on the left ankle. The man asks the store owner about the ribbons.

"Oh, this is a specially trained parrot. If you tug on the red ribbon the parrot will recite the Declaration of Independence. If you tug on the blue ribbon he recites the Gettysburg Address."

"That's pretty awesome," the man responds, "but what happens if you tug both at the same time?"

The parrot answers the man, "I'd fall off my perch, you moron."

✳ A MAN BUYS A CHAINSAW from a hardware store. The salesman tells the man the chainsaw is the most powerful saw on the market. It will take down any tree in a matter of minutes. The man falls for the sales pitch and takes the chainsaw home. He returns the next day with the chainsaw and a huge complaint.

"You lied," the customer barks. "I started cutting down a tree in my yard at noon and the thing didn't come down until after 6 P.M. It took forever."

"That's crazy," the salesman replies. "There must be an issue. Let me take a look at it." The salesman grabs the chainsaw and pulls the cord. The chainsaw rips to life.

"Jesus!" the customer yells over the sound, with his hands over his ears. "What is that noise?"

Transportation

✳ A TAXI PASSENGER TAPS THE driver on the shoulder to ask him a question about the city. The driver screams, loses control of the car, nearly hits a bus, drives up on the sidewalk, and stops the car inches before it crashes through the front of a store window. Both men sit completely silent until the driver turns and says, "Look man, don't *ever* do that to me again. You scared the crap out of me!"

The passenger apologizes and says, "I didn't realize that a little tap would scare you so much."

The driver replies, "Sorry, it's not really your fault. Today is my first day as a cab driver. Before this I drove a hearse."

✱ A TRAIN CONDUCTOR IS COLLECTING tickets and comes across a drunk man asleep in his seat. The conductor asks the man for his ticket, but the drunk can't find it in any of his pockets.

"That's all right," says the conductor, "I'm sure you paid for the ticket."

"I'm not worried about that," the drunk responds. "If I can't find my ticket, how will I remember where the hell I'm going?"

✱ TWO PILOTS ARE IN A small aircraft. Suddenly both engines shut off, and the plane goes into a spiraling nosedive. Panicking, the copilot says to the pilot, "If this keeps up, do you think we'll fall out?"

The pilot pulls back on the handles and says, "I should hope not, buddy, we've been friends for years."

✱ A DAILY COMMUTER APPROACHES THE conductor of a train. "Excuse me," the commuter begins, "this morning I brought a bottle of Scotch on the train. It was a gift for a coworker who retired today. When I got into the office this morning, I realized I left it on the train. Didn't anyone return it?"

"No," says the conductor, "but someone turned in the guy who found it."

✱ SHORTLY AFTER A BRITISH AIRWAYS flight had reached its cruising altitude, the captain announces: "Ladies and gentlemen, this is your captain. Welcome to Flight 293, nonstop from London Heathrow to Toronto. The weather ahead is good, so we should have a smooth, uneventful flight. So sit back, relax, and *oh my god!*" Silence follows. Some moments later the captain comes back on the intercom. "Ladies and gentlemen. I'm sorry if I scared you. While I was talking to you, a flight attendant accidentally spilled a cup of hot coffee in my lap. You should see the front of my pants!"

One passenger yells, "You should see the back of mine!"

✱ A TRUCK DRIVER IS HAVING breakfast at a diner when three menacing bikers enter through the front door. It's obvious the bikers are drunk and looking for a fight. They surround the truck driver. The first biker spits in the man's eggs. The second biker pours orange juice over the truck driver's head. The third biker pulls out his stool so he falls on the floor. The man says nothing, stands up, and walks out of the diner.

"Not much of a man," the first biker says to the waitress.

"No," says the waitress, "and not much of a driver either. He didn't even see your bikes parked in front of his truck and he just ran right over them."

 Famous Funnies

"Recession is when a neighbor loses his job. Depression is when you lose yours."—Ronald Reagan

Armed Services and Law Enforcement

✳ A DRILL SERGEANT IS YELLING at one of the young men in his battalion. "I didn't see you at camouflage training this afternoon, Private!" the drill sergeant barks. "Well thank you very much, Sarge!" the private answers proudly.

✳ THE JUDGE STARES DOWN A man standing in front of his bench.

"You look incredibly familiar," the judge tells the defendant. "Have you been here before?"

"No, your honor," the man replies. "I'm your son's music teacher. I'm the person who encouraged him to take up the drums."

The judge yells to the sheriff's officers, "Throw him in jail!"

✳ THE HARDEST PART ABOUT LIVING on a submarine captain's salary is trying to keep your head above water.

✳ A GROUP OF NEW POLICE officers are in a training class, where they're learning how to take custody of a suspect.

"You have to be ready for any situation," the chief tells his new class. "For example, Officer Jones, what would you do if you had to arrest your own mother?"

Officer Jones answers quickly, "I'd call for backup!"

✸ THE LOCAL SHERIFF'S OFFICE IS looking for a new deputy. Dan, who is not exactly the smartest guy in town, goes in to try out for the job.

"Okay," the sheriff asks, "what is one and one?"

"Eleven," Dan replies.

The sheriff thinks to himself, "That's not exactly what I meant, but he's right."

The sheriff continues, "What two days of the week start with the letter 'T'?"

"Today and tomorrow," Dan answers.

The sheriff is again surprised that Dan supplied an answer that wasn't correct, but one that he had never thought of himself.

"Final question, so listen carefully. Who killed Abraham Lincoln?"

Dan looks a little surprised, then thinks really hard for a minute and finally admits, "I really don't know."

"Well, why don't you go home and work on that one for a while? If you figure it out, give me a call."

Dan wanders over to the bar where his friend is waiting to hear the results of the interview.

"How'd it go?" his friend asks.

"It went great! I didn't even get the job yet and I'm already working on a murder case!"

✸ AN ADMIRAL IS STARING OFF the deck of his battleship at the approaching enemy on the horizon.

"Fetch my red shirt," the admiral says to his first officer. "If I'm wounded in battle I don't want the men to see I'm bleeding. It will kill morale."

"But sir," says the first officer, "there is a fleet of fifteen ships coming right for us." "Oh," the admiral sighs. "Well, in that case go grab my brown pants."

✳ A BANK ROBBER HAS HIT the same bank three times in a month. An FBI agent is questioning all of the bank employees in an attempt to keep it from happening a fourth time.

The FBI agent asks a new teller, "Have you noticed anything in particular about the robber? You have seen him three times now."

"Yes," the teller replies, "now that you mention it, I did notice something—every time he comes back to rob the bank he's much better dressed."

✳ A HEARTLESS DRILL INSTRUCTOR SCREAMED at his platoon for over an hour. He got in the face of a private and yelled, "I bet when I die you'll show up at my grave and spit on it!"

"Not me," the private said. "After I get out of the army I'm never standing in a line again."

✳ THE WARDEN OF A HIGH-SECURITY prison brings one of the inmates into his office. The inmate had started a riot that morning.

"I've got two questions," the warden says sternly. "Why were you revolting and how did you get out of your cell?"

The prisoner looks the warden in the eye and tells him, "I'm revolting because the prison food is awful and inedible."

"I understand," the warden replies, "and how did you break the locks on the cell door?" The prisoner answers, "I used the scrambled eggs."

✳ A DRUNK DRIVER IS PULLED over by a state trooper. The state trooper asks the man, "Have you been drinking tonight, sir?"

The drunk man looks around his car and replies, "How did you know? Is there an ugly woman in my car?"

✳ A DEFENDANT STANDS BEFORE THE judge. "Before we begin, defendant, how do you plead?"

"That depends," says the accused man.

"Depends on what?" the judge asks.

"It depends on what they've got as evidence against me."

✳ A COP PULLS OVER A woman going the wrong way down a one-way street.

"Where the heck do you think you're going?" the cop asks.

"I don't know, but I must be late because it looks like everyone is coming back."

Odd Jobs

✳ A MAN IS SITTING AT a bar enjoying a cocktail when an exceptionally gorgeous, sexy young woman enters. The man can't stop staring at her. The young woman notices this and walks directly toward him. Before he can offer his apologies for being so rude, the young woman says to him, "I'll do anything you want me to do, no matter how kinky, for $100, with one condition."

Flabbergasted, the man asks what the condition is.

The young woman replies, "You have to tell me what you want me to do in just three words."

The man considers her proposition for a moment, withdraws his wallet from his pocket, and hands the woman five twenty-dollar bills. He looks deeply into her eyes and slowly says, "Paint my house."

✳ DID YOU HEAR ABOUT THE woman who tried to make a career out of being a gold digger? It didn't really pan out.

✳ DID YOU HEAR ABOUT THE man who got a job as a human cannonball? He was so excited he went ballistic.

✳ HOW DID THE CIRCUS OWNER get so rich? He spent years paying his employees peanuts.

✳ WHY IS IT SO HARD for dwarves to get work? Employers don't like paying people under the table.

✳ DID YOU HEAR ABOUT THE family that was so poor that a burglar broke into their home and all he got was practice?

✳ A CANNIBAL COMES HOME FROM work and tells his wife he brought an old friend home with him to eat. "That's great," says the wife. "Just put him in the freezer and we'll have him next week."

✳ A HUMAN CANNONBALL HAS HAD enough of the terrible working conditions, so he decides to quit the circus. He breaks the news to the owner of the circus after the final performance of the night.

"You can't quit the circus!" the owner cries. "Where am I going to find a man of your caliber?"

✳ A PIRATE PAYS A VISIT to his favorite bar. The bartender says, "Hey, I haven't seen you in a while! You look awful! What the heck happened?"

"I'm fine," the pirate replies.

"What about that wooden leg? What happened?"

"Oh that," says the pirate. "Well, we got into a fight at sea and a cannonball hit my leg. The ship's doctor fixed me up with a wooden leg to replace the one I lost."

"Well, what about that hook on your hand? The last time you were in for drinks you had both hands."

"Well in that same battle we commandeered the enemy ship. The enemy took off my hand in a sword fight but the doctor saved me again. Gave me this hook to replace my hand."

"Okay," says the bartender, "what's with the eye patch? Let me guess—you lost it in the same battle."

"Um, no. The other day a bird flying over the ship crapped in my eye."

"You're kidding," says the bartender. "You lost an eye because of bird crap?"

"Well, not really," the pirate answers, embarrassed. "I really wasn't used to the hook yet."

✳ A CHURCH PUTS AN AD in the newspaper for a person to ring the bell in the belfry on Sunday mornings. No one applies for the position except for a young man with no arms. The church administrator isn't sure he can handle the job, but the man climbs the tower and rings the bell using just his head. On his first Sunday on the job, the man gets a little too excited and hits the bell a little too hard with his melon. He falls from the belfry and lands on the church steps. Two parishioners late for services rush past him.

"Who was that guy?" the wife asks her husband as they enter the church.

"I'm not sure," the husband replies, "but his face does ring a bell."

✱ TWO COWBOYS ARE RIDING THROUGH a canyon when off in the distance they hear the sound of Indian drums. One cowboy says to the other, "I don't like the sound of those drums!" From across the canyon a voice calls out, "He's not our normal drummer!"

✱ WHY DON'T MANY ONE-ARMED MEN work as butlers? They can take it, but they can't dish it out.

Miscellaneous Jobs

✱ WHY DID THE WEATHERMAN TAKE a leave of absence after breaking both arms and both legs? He would have trouble working with the four casts.

✱ WHY DON'T MANY PEOPLE GO into the funeral business? Because opening a parlor is a huge undertaking.

✱ A COLLEGE PROFESSOR WAS VERY worried about his recent study on earthquakes. It turns out his findings were on shaky ground.

✱ ELIAS HOWARD IS CREDITED WITH being the inventor of the zipper, but most of his friends called him the lord of the flies.

✱ WHY ARE PHOTOGRAPHERS ALWAYS SO depressed? Because they don't do anything all day but focus on the negatives.

✱ A MAN GOES TO GET his haircut and the barber asks, "Should I cut the hair in back?"

The man replies, "What's wrong with doing it right here in the chair?"

✱ DID YOU HEAR THAT EVERYONE at the mint went on strike? They wanted to make less money.

 Famous Funnies

"I always wanted to be somebody, but now I realize I should have been more specific."—Lily Tomlin

✱ WHAT DID ONE GEOLOGIST SAY to the other while they both stared down at a giant fissure in the rocks? "I wonder whose fault this is."

✱ A WOMAN IS AMAZED BY the pastor who lives next door and how quickly he changes his personality. Around the neighborhood, he is incredibly shy, quiet, and timid. As soon as he begins to preach, he becomes loud, boisterous, and is able to entertain the congregation with his sermons.

"I'm not sure how you go from one personality to the next," the woman tells the pastor over coffee.

"Oh, it's simple," the pastor explains. "That guy in church is my altar ego."

✱ A YOUNG MAN IS FIRED from his job after asking customers if they wanted "smoking or nonsmoking." He was fired because the correct terminology in the funeral home business is "cremation or burial."

✱ UNABLE TO READ THE NAME on the label of package, a postman decides that the weight of the box and the words left on the ripped label mean the package is for the local book shop. "I've got a package that I think is for you," the mailman tells the store owner.

"Well, what's the name on the label?" the store owner asks.

"That's the problem. It's obliterated."

"Well it can't be for me," the store owner answers. "My name is John."

✳ A YOUNG MAN WALKS INTO a bar and says, "Bartender, a round of drinks for everyone, on me!"

The bartender says, "Wow, that's very generous, why the good mood?"

The man replies, "You bet I'm in a good mood! I just got hired by the city to go around to every parking meter in town and remove all the money. I start on Monday!"

The bartender congratulates him on the new job and hands out drinks to every customer. Monday evening arrives and the man returns to the bar and says, "Bartender, two rounds for everyone in the bar, on me!"

The bartender says, "Whoa! This new job has got you in a generous mood. I can't imagine what you'll do when you finally get your first paycheck!"

The man looks at the bartender with a wondering look on his face. He reaches into his pocket, pulls out a handful of quarters, throws them on the bar, and asks, "You mean they're going to pay me, too?"

✳ A TOUR GUIDE IS LEADING a group through a museum in London. "This mummy here is over 5,000 years old," the guide tells the group. "It's possible that Moses saw it."

A tourist raises her hand and asks, "When was Moses ever in London?"

✳ WHAT DID THE MATH GRADUATE say to the history graduate? "Can I get two orders of fries, please?"

✱ STEPHEN IS GETTING HIS HAIR cut when he tells the barber he is going to Rome on vacation the next day.

"Who knows," Stephen says, "I might even get to meet the Pope."

"You'll never meet the Pope," the barber laughs. "He doesn't mix with the common people anymore."

"You never know," says Stephen, "strange things happen."

"It will never happen," the barber snaps, "and I'm so sure it won't happen I'll bet you $100 it won't happen."

Stephen agrees. A month later, Stephen returns to get his hair cut and tells the barber all about his vacation.

"And you owe me $100," Stephen tells the barber while handing him a picture of himself and the Pope.

"My God!" the barber exclaims. "How did that happen?"

"It was amazing," Stephen begins. "I was walking through St. Peter's Square when the Pope spotted me from his balcony and summoned me to the Vatican, because he had a question to ask."

"What did he ask?" says the barber.

"He said, 'My son, where in God's name did you get that terrible haircut?'"

✱ DID YOU HEAR ABOUT THE farmer who won an award from the U.S. Department of Agriculture? He was outstanding in his field.

✱ A CONSTRUCTION WORKER ACCIDENTALLY CUTS off one of his ears with an electric saw. He calls out to a guy walking on the street below, "Hey, do you see my ear down there?"

The guy on the street picks up an ear. "Is this it?"

"No," replies the construction worker, "mine had a pencil behind it."

✱ WHAT DID THE FIREMAN NAME his two sons? Jose and Jose B.

✱ TWO FACTORY WORKERS ARE TALKING. The woman says, "I can make the boss give me the day off."

The man asks, "And how would you do that?"

The woman says, "Just wait and see."

She then hangs upside down from the ceiling.

The boss comes in and asks, "What are you doing?"

The woman replies, "I'm a light bulb."

The boss then says, "You've been working so much that you've gone crazy. I think you need to take the day off."

The man starts to follow her and the boss says, "Where are you going?"

The man says, "I'm going home, too. How am I supposed to work in the dark?"

✱ DID YOU HEAR ABOUT THE painter who kept getting fired for dropping things on people? He couldn't hold his lacquer.

✱ A SCIENTIST WORKED AWAY IN obscurity for years with peculiar experiments on spiders. After years and years he placed an advertisement in several academic journals to let the community know he was ready to host a live show to demonstrate his findings. Hundreds came to the event, more out of curiosity than anything else, since details of the findings were kept secret. The scientist took the stage and said, "Today I will demonstrate two things. First, spiders can understand and respond to basic commands."

The crowd laughed and jeered. Undeterred, he opened a box on his desk and a spider crawled out.

"Spider, walk left," the scientist said. The spider moved to its left. The crowd was silenced.

"Spider, move right." The spider moved right.

The crowd gasped. Forward, backward, the spider responded again and again. The crowd applauded in awe. The scientist then removed all of the spider's legs. The crowd, confused by this, watched in silence.

"Move left." The spider didn't move. "Move right." Nothing. Forward, backward, no response.

"This is to demonstrate my second finding. Once you remove a spider's legs, it goes deaf."

✳ TWO PAINTERS PAINT A HOUSE and hand the customer the bill. The customer notices that the men charged no money for the actual paint. The customer says, "You guys did such a good job. Why aren't you charging me for the paint?"

The head painter looks at the man and says, "Don't worry about the paint, it's on the house."

✳ A VERY SUCCESSFUL LAWYER BUYS a new Ferrari. He parks in front of his office, ready to show it off to his colleagues. As he gets out, a truck passes too close and completely tears the door off of the driver's side. The counselor immediately grabs his cell phone, dials 911, and within minutes a policeman pulls up to take a report. Before the officer has a chance to ask any questions, the lawyer starts screaming hysterically. His Ferrari, which he had just picked up the day before, was now completely ruined and would never be the same, no matter what the body shop did to it. When the lawyer finally winds down from his ranting and raving, the officer shakes his head in disgust.

"I can't believe how materialistic you lawyers are," he says. "All you care about is money and your possessions."

The lawyer unleashes a stream of obscenities before the officer can calm him down. "Hear me out . . . see, you are so worried about your car, you didn't even notice that the accident took off your left arm."

"Oh my god!" screams the lawyer. "Where's my Rolex?"

✳ A CLIENT RECEIVES HIS BILL from his lawyer in the mail. He's livid at the amount and calls the lawyer to berate him for charging such ridiculous fees. The lawyer listens for a moment before stopping the client mid-sentence.

"You know," the lawyer says, "you're being a real jerk about this and I'm beginning to regret naming my first boat after you."

✳ OLD BANKERS NEVER DIE. THEY just lose interest.

CHAPTER 6

Politics and Historical Events

Groucho Marx, an American comedian, once said, "Politics is the art of looking for trouble, finding it everywhere, diagnosing it incorrectly, and applying the wrong remedies." It's amazing to think that an observation made more than fifty years ago about the politics of the time is still relevant today. Sad, but true. Since you can't do much to change the government, there is little left to do but laugh at the men and women in charge.

❋ HOW MANY GOVERNMENT WORKERS DOES it take to change a light bulb? Two: one to insist the light bulb has been taken care of and the other to screw it into a faucet.

 Famous Funnies

> "You can lead a man to Congress, but you can't make him think."—
> Milton Berle

❋ IT'S ONLY NATURAL THAT ALL politicians have a God complex. They haven't done anything in ages, they give all the best jobs to their immediate family, and no one really believes in them.

✸ A TOP OFFICIAL IN THE Democratic Party leaves his office to check out a local Republican rally. While he's spying from afar, a mugger approaches and holds him up at gunpoint. He returns to his office, upset and despondent over what happened. He explains the entire story to his assistant.

"Weren't there cops around?" the assistant asks.

"Of course," the Democrat replies.

"Well then, why didn't you yell out for help?" the assistant asks.

"What?" he shoots back. "And have Republicans think I was cheering for them?"

✸ DURING HIS PRESIDENCY, GEORGE W. Bush secretly bombed the Canary Islands in an attempt to stop the spread of bird flu. His cabinet stopped him before he could do the same to Turkey.

✸ THE PRESIDENT WAS AWAKENED IN the middle of the night by a call from the Pentagon. "Mr. President," the four-star general began, "I've got good news and bad news."

"What's the bad news?" the president asked.

"The country is being taken over by aliens from another planet." "My God," the president said. "What's the good news?" "The good news is," said the general, "they pee oil and they've eaten Rush Limbaugh."

 Comedy Facts

The record for most comedy specials by one comic is held by Kathy Griffin with twenty. In her career, Griffin has had one half-hour special, eighteen one-hour specials, and a two-hour special.

✸ GEORGE WASHINGTON, ABRAHAM LINCOLN, AND George Bush are in a plane. The pilot says that the plane must lighten its load. So the three presidents decide to drop one item each. George Washington drops a quarter. Abe Lincoln drops a penny. George Bush drops a live grenade. When the presidents land, they visit the area where they dropped their items to make sure no serious damage was done. They find a man holding his head and cursing. George Washington asks the man what's wrong.

"I was walking down the street when a quarter falls from the sky and hits me on the top of the head!"

The presidents continue down the road and find another man hopping on one foot and cursing.

Abe Lincoln asks, "What happened?"

"I was standing on my porch when a penny fell from the sky and hit my big toe!"

The presidents continue on to find a young boy laughing hysterically in his front yard while his house burns to the ground.

George Bush asks, "What's so funny?"

The boy replies, "I just farted and my house exploded!"

 ## Comedy Facts

In the late 1950s and early 1960s, stand-up comedians such as Mort Sahl began developing their acts in small folk clubs in major cities, including San Francisco, Los Angeles, and New York. Taking notice of the political and social changes of that time, comedians began commenting on and poking fun at issues of the day like race relations, sex, religion, and drugs. Comedians also began pushing the boundaries with language.

✱ A TOUR GUIDE IS LEADING a group around the Washington, D.C., area when they come to a spot on the Potomac River.

"This is where George Washington allegedly threw a dollar across the river," the guide tells the group.

"That's impossible," says one skeptical tourist. "No one could ever throw a dollar that far."

The guide tells the man, "Well, you have to keep in mind that money went a lot farther in those days."

✳ ON HIS DEATHBED, A LIFELONG Republican told his best friend that he was switching parties and becoming a Democrat.

"My God," his friend replied, "why would you do such a thing?"

"Simple," the man muttered in his last breath, "because I'd rather one of them die than one of us."

 Famous Funnies

> "The reason there are two senators for each state is so that one can be the designated driver."—Jay Leno

✳ WHY DON'T POLITICIANS LISTEN TO their conscience? They don't like taking advice from complete strangers.

✳ A LOCAL CONGRESSMAN WAS SITTING in his office when the phone rang. He picked it up, said little, smiled widely, said "Thank you," and hung up the phone.

He picked the phone back up to call his mother. "Mom, it's me," he said. "I won the election!"

"Honestly?" she said in response to the news.

"Does it really matter how I did it?" he replied.

✳ TWO PRESIDENTIAL AIDES ARE HAVING coffee in a back room at the White House. "Sometimes I wish we worked for the pope and not the president," one of them says.

"Why?" asks the second aide.

"Because then we'd only have to kiss his ring."

✳ FLYING ACROSS THE COUNTRY IN Air Force One, the president jokes with his staff.

"I'm thinking about tossing a $100 bill out the window and making someone very happy."

A White House aide comments, "Why don't you throw twenty $100 bills out the window and make twenty people happy?"

Another staffer jokes, "Why don't you throw a hundred $100 bills out the window and make a hundred people happy?"

A member of the plane staff, wanting to get in on the act, chimes in and says, "Why don't you throw yourself out the window and make half the country happy?"

✳ WHILE WAITING FOR A WHITE House press conference to begin, a journalist turns to the stranger to his right and asks, "Did you hear the latest joke about the president?"

"Before you continue," says the stranger, "I should tell you I'm part of the White House staff."

"Okay, thanks," the journalist responds. "Then I'll tell the joke a little slower than normal."

✳ LAURA BUSH TELLS GEORGE W. Bush, "We have this weekend free. What should we do?"

"Well, let's think," he responds.

Laura replies, "No, let's do something we both can do."

 Famous Funnies

> "Hillary Clinton says she's the most qualified because she was married to a president for eight years. Now let me ask you, if a brain surgeon quit his job, would everyone in the operating room say, 'Wait, let's get his wife'?"—Jackie Mason

✳ HILLARY CLINTON DIES AND GOES to heaven. St. Peter is giving her a tour of heaven when she notices that there are dozens of clocks on the wall. Each clock displays a different time of day. When she asks St. Peter about the clocks, he replies, "We have a clock for each person on earth, and every time that person tells a lie the hands move. The clock ticks off one second each time a lie is told."

Special attention is given to two clocks. The clock belonging to Mother Teresa has never moved, indicating that she never told a lie.

The clock for Abraham Lincoln has only moved twice. He only told two lies in his life.

Hillary asks, "Where is Bill's clock?"

St. Peter replies, "Jesus has it in his office. He's using it as a ceiling fan."

✳ PLENTY OF AMERICANS DON'T TRUST Barack Obama because they claim he's not a "real American" like they are. They have a point; they aren't like him. He's too thin.

✳ HOW MANY POLITICIANS DOES IT take to change a light bulb? Two—one to change the light bulb and then one to change it back again after he gets elected.

✳ A REPUBLICAN, A DEMOCRAT, AND Bill Clinton are traveling in a car when a tornado picks up the car and tosses them miles into the air. When the car finally comes back down, the three men realize they've been transported to Oz.

"I'm going to ask the Wizard for a brain," says the Democrat.

"I'm going to ask him for a heart," says the Republican.

Bill Clinton looks around and asks the two men, "Where do you think Dorothy is?"

✳ BARACK OBAMA IS SKATING ON a frozen pond not far from the White House. The pond cracks and Obama falls in. Two boys skating on the same pond rush over and pull the president from the icy water.

"Boys," Obama says, "you saved my life. How can I ever repay you?"

The first boy thinks about it and says, "I'd like to tour the White House and go in all the rooms."

Obama agrees.

"I'd like a motorized wheelchair," the second boy requests of the president.

"A wheelchair? Why do you need a wheelchair?" the president asks. "Well," the boy explains, "when my old man finds out I rescued you from drowning, he's gonna break both my legs."

✳ THE PRESIDENT OF THE UNITED States wanted a special postage stamp issued, with his picture on it. He expressed his wish to the postmaster general and stressed that the stamp should be of the highest quality. After the stamps were released, the president immediately began hearing complaints that they were not sticking properly. He was furious. He called the postmaster general, who checked out the issue at several post offices and then reported on the problem to the president.

"Mr. President," the postmaster told the commander in chief on the phone, "the stamp is really of fine quality. The problem is it's just not sticking to envelopes. But we think we've pinpointed the problem."

"And what's that?" the president asked.

"Well," the postmaster said sheepishly, "people keep spitting on the side with your face on it."

 ## Ask the Comedian

Is it really possible to make a living at telling jokes?
Absolutely. Think of all the stand-up comics mentioned throughout this book. It might not be possible to become a world-famous comedian or comedy writer, but there are countless people who make a career of traveling the United States performing comedy in clubs and restaurants and even at corporate events. As with any job, you'll get back the commitment you put into it.

✳ A LADY BUYS A NEW $100,000 Mercedes and proudly drives it off the showroom floor to take home. Halfway home, she attempts to change radio stations and finds that there appears to be only one station. She immediately turns around and heads back to the dealer. Once at the dealership, she finds her salesman and explains that her radio is not working, and they must replace it since she only has one radio station. The salesman calms her down and tells her that her car radio is voice-activated; she will only need to state aloud the type of music she wants and the radio will find it. She gets into the car, starts the engine, says the word "country," and the radio changes to a station playing a George Strait song. She is satisfied and starts home.

After a while she decides to try out the radio again and says "rock 'n' roll." The radio station changes and a song by the Rolling Stones comes from the speakers. Quite pleased, the woman continues driving. A few blocks from her house, another driver runs a light, causing her to slam on her brakes to avoid a collision. The woman angrily exclaims, "Moron!" The radio immediately switches over to the president's press conference.

✱ TWO POLITICIANS ARE HAVING LUNCH. The first politician says, "There are many ways of making money, but there is only one honest way."

"And how's that?" the second politician asks.

The first politician laughs and replies, "I have no idea. I thought maybe you would."

✱ DID YOU HEAR THAT THE George W. Bush Presidential Library burned to the ground in a fire? Unfortunately, all three books were lost, and one of them was barely all colored in.

✱ BILL CLINTON AND HIS PERSONAL driver are cruising along a country road one night when all of a sudden they hit a pig. The impact kills the pig instantly. Bill tells his driver to go up to the farmhouse and explain to the owners what happened, and that it was a complete accident. About an hour later, the driver staggers back to the car with a bottle of wine in one hand, a cigar in the other, and his clothes all ripped and torn.

"What happened to you?" asks Bill.

"Well, the farmer gave me the wine, his wife gave me the cigar, and his nineteen-year-old daughter made mad, passionate love to me," says the driver. "We spent the last hour celebrating."

"Celebrating?" Clinton asks. "What did you tell them that had them celebrating?"

The driver replies, "I knocked on the front door and said, 'I'm Bill Clinton's personal driver and I just killed the pig.'"

✳ A LIBERAL CAME UPON A genie and said, "You're a genie. Can you grant me three wishes?"

The genie replied, "Yes, but only if you're feeling generous enough to share your good fortune."

The liberal said, "I'm a liberal. I'm always happy to share."

The genie said, "Okay then, whatever you wish for, I'll give every conservative in the country two of it. What's your first wish?"

"I would like a new sports car."

"Okay, you've got it, and every conservative in the country gets two sports cars. What's your second wish?"

"I'd like a million dollars."

"Okay, you get a million dollars, every conservative gets two million dollars. What's your third and final wish?"

"Well, I've always wanted to donate a kidney."

 Famous Funnies

> "It's so cold here in Washington, D.C., that politicians have their hands in their own pockets."—Bob Hope

✳ A MAN AND HIS WIFE are discussing what they think their son will be when he grows up.

"I have an idea," says the father. He puts a ten-dollar bill, a bottle of whiskey, and a Bible on the coffee table. "If he takes the money, he'll be a banker. If he takes the whiskey, he'll be a wino, and if he takes the Bible, that means he'll be a preacher."

So the man and his wife hide just before their son comes in the door, and watch from where they're hiding. The boy saunters over to the coffee table. He picks up the ten-dollar bill, looks at it, then sets it down. He picks up the bottle of whiskey, uncorks it, sniffs it, then sets it down. He picks up the Bible, leafs through it, and sets it down. Then the boy takes the money and stuffs it into his pocket, grabs the whiskey, and walks off with the Bible under his arm.

"Well how do you like that!" exclaims the father. "He's going to be a politician!"

✳ RICHARD NIXON, JIMMY CARTER, AND Bill Clinton are among the passengers on a boat that's about to sink. As the ship begins to capsize, Carter yells, "Quick, save the women and children!"

Nixon replies, "Screw the women!"

Clinton wonders out loud, "Do we have time for that?"

✳ A THIEF STICKS A GUN into a man's ribs and says, "Give me your money, now!"

The man, shocked by the sudden attack, replies, "You can't do this to me. I'm a congressman!"

The thief replies, "Oh, well in that case, give me *my* money!"

✳ WHY DID GEORGE WASHINGTON HAVE trouble sleeping? Because he found it impossible to lie.

✳ HOW MANY POLITICIANS DOES IT take to screw in a light bulb? One, but boy does it get screwed good.

✳ WHAT HAPPENS WHEN YOU MATE a pig with a politician? Nothing, because there are some things even a pig won't do.

✳ BILL AND HILLARY ARE FAST asleep in the First Bedroom, when Hillary wakes and starts shaking Bill. Bill groggily opens his eyes and says, "Honey, it's 3 A.M. What do you want?"

"I have to use the bathroom," Hillary replies.

Bill responds, "Please tell me you didn't wake me up just to tell me you have to go to the bathroom."

"No," Hillary says. "I just wanted to tell you to save my spot."

✻ WHY WERE THE EARLY DAYS of history called the Dark Ages? Because there were so many knights.

✻ WHICH ENGLISH KING INVENTED THE fireplace? Alfred the Grate.

✻ HOW WAS THE ROMAN EMPIRE cut in half? With a pair of Caesars.

✻ WHAT KIND OF LIGHTING DID Noah use for the ark? Floodlights and ark lights.

✻ A MEMBER OF THE SENATE, known for his hot temper, explodes one day in mid-session and begins to shout, "Half of this Senate is made up of cowards and corrupt politicians!" All the other senators demand that the angry member withdraw his statement or be removed for the remainder of the session. After a moment to think, the angry senator apologizes. "I'm sorry," he says. "What I meant to say was half of this Senate is *not* made up of cowards and corrupt politicians!"

✻ TWO YOUNG BOYS ARE TALKING before school.
  "My uncle ran for Senate last year," the first boy says to his classmate.
  "Really?" the second boy asks. "What does he do now?"
  "Nothing," the first boy explains. "He got elected."

✻ HOW DO YOU KEEP VICE President Joe Biden busy until lunch? Tell him to stand in the corner of the Oval Office.

✻ WHO IS THE MOST POWERFUL individual in Washington, D.C.? The president's dog—he can get the president to kneel in front of him.

✻ WHY SHOULD ALL FORMER SENATORS be buried 100 feet deep when they die? Because deep down, they're really good people.

✻ HOW DID GEORGE WASHINGTON SPEAK to his army? In general terms.

✷ "YOU SHOULD BE ASHAMED," A father tells his young son. "When Abraham Lincoln was your age, he used to walk ten miles every day to get to school."

"Really?" the son responds. "Well, when he was your age, he was president."

 ## Comedy Facts

The Guinness World Record for the longest stand-up comedy show is 80 hours. Over 130 comedians performed over two days at the Laugh Factory in Hollywood, California.

✷ WHAT ARE THE INGREDIENTS FOR the homemade Bill Clinton stew? One wiener, one cooked goose, lots of spilled beans, and tons of hot water.

✷ IN AN AMERICAN HISTORY DISCUSSION group, a professor is trying to explain how society's idea of beauty changes with time. "For example," he says, "the winner of the Miss America pageant in 1921 stood five foot one, weighed only 108 pounds, and had measurements of 30-25-32. How do you think she'd do in today's version of the contest?"

The class is silent until one woman comments, "She'd lose for sure."

"Why is that?" asks the professor.

"Well for one thing," the student answers, "she's probably dead."

✷ HILLARY CLINTON GOES IN FOR her annual gynecological exam. The doctor tells her she's pregnant. Hillary storms out of the office and calls Bill.

"You got me pregnant! How could you be so careless?"

After a moment of stunned silence, Bill asks, "Who is this?"

✱ BEFORE HIS INAUGURATION, GEORGE W. Bush was invited to take a tour of the White House. After drinking several glasses of water, he asked President Clinton if he could use the bathroom in the Oval Office. He was astonished to see that the president had a solid gold urinal installed. That night, George W. told his wife, Laura, about the urinal.

"Just think," he said, "when I'm president, I'll have my own personal gold urinal!"

Laura had lunch with Hillary Clinton on her tour of the White House and told her how impressed George had been with his discovery of the president's private bathroom and gold urinal.

"Bill doesn't have a gold urinal," Hillary told Laura, "but that explains who peed in Bill's saxophone."

✱ A WASHINGTON, D.C., COP PULLS Jenna Bush over for speeding and notices her eyes are red and bloodshot.

The officer says, "Your eyes look red. Have you been drinking?"

Jenna replies, "No, officer, but your eyes look a little glazed. Have you been eating doughnuts?"

✱ A REPORTER CORNERS GEORGE W. Bush at a press conference after his election. "Many people feel the only reason you were elected president is because of the enormous power and influence of your father."

"That notion is ridiculous!" says Bush. "It doesn't matter how powerful the man is. He was only allowed to vote once!"

✱ IF "PROS" ARE THE OPPOSITE of "cons," does that mean "congress" is the opposite of "progress"?

✱ PRESIDENT GEORGE BUSH WALKS INTO the Oval Office and sees Vice President Dan Quayle celebrating wildly.

"What's going on, Mr. Quayle?" the president inquires.

"I just done finished a jigsaw puzzle in record time!" the vice president beams.

"How long did it take you?" President Bush asks.

"I did it in just over a month," Quayle explains, "but the box said it would take 3–5 years!"

* A MAN IS SITTING AT a bar during a costume party when a friend comes up to him and says, "You were supposed to dress up like something that symbolizes your love life."

"I am," the man says.

"You look like Abe Lincoln," the friend responds.

"Yup," he replies, taking a sip of beer. "My last four scores were seven years ago."

* A HISTORY TEACHER IS DISCUSSING George Washington with his class. "George Washington not only chopped down his father's cherry tree," the teacher explains, "but also admitted to doing it. Does anyone know why his father didn't punish him?"

A girl in the front of the class answers, "Maybe because George still had the axe in his hand?"

* WHY'S RICHARD NIXON LIKE AN old collector's item? Both are worth more in the box.

* ONE NIGHT, GEORGE W. BUSH is awakened by George Washington's ghost in the White House. President Bush asks him, "George, what is the best thing I could do to help the country?"

"Set an honest and honorable example, just as I did," Washington advises.

The next night, the ghost of Thomas Jefferson appears in the Oval Office.

"Tom," Bush asks, "what is the best thing I could do to help the country?"

Jefferson advises Bush, "Cut taxes and reduce the size of government."

Bush stays awake the next night and Abraham Lincoln's ghost appears.

"Abe," Bush says. "What is the best thing I could do to help the country?"

Honest Abe answers, "Take the night off and go see a play."

✳ LITTLE BILLY WANTS SIXTY-FIVE DOLLARS for a new video game. He prays for two weeks, but nothing happens. He decides to write God a letter requesting the money. When the postal authorities receive the letter addressed to God, USA, they decide to send it to the president. The president is so impressed, touched, and amused that he instructs his secretary to send Billy five dollars. Little Billy is delighted with the five dollars and sits down to write a thank-you note to God. His letter says, "Dear God, Thank you very much for sending the money, however, I noticed that for some reason you had to send it through Washington, D.C., and, as usual, those crooks deducted sixty dollars. Thanks anyway, Billy."

✳ PRESIDENT OBAMA GOES TO VISIT the Queen of England. As Air Force One arrives at Heathrow Airport, President Obama is warmly welcomed by the Queen. They are driven in a car to the edge of central London, where they get into a magnificent seventeenth-century carriage hitched to six white horses. They continue on toward Buckingham Palace and wave to the crowds gathered to greet them. Suddenly the right rear horse lets out the loudest fart ever heard in the British Empire. The smell is awful and both passengers put handkerchiefs over their noses. The two dignitaries of state do their best to ignore the incident. Because the smell lingers, the Queen feels she must say something. She turns to President Obama and says, "Mr. President, please accept my regrets. I am sure you understand there are some things that even a Queen cannot control."

Obama looks at her and replies, "Your Majesty, I completely understand. Until you mentioned it, I thought it was one of the horses."

✳ DID YOU HEAR THE RUMOR that the president was poisoned last week but doctors were able to find a cure? The information is purely antidotal.

✱ AIR FORCE ONE CRASHES ON a farm in the middle of rural Kentucky. The local sheriff's department mobilizes and descends on the farm in force. By the time authorities arrive, the aircraft is totally destroyed with only a burned hull left. The sheriff and his men approach the smoking mess and find no remains. They spot the farmer plowing a field not too far away. He acts as if nothing has happened. The sheriff hurries over to the farmer's tractor and yells, "Hank! Did you see this terrible accident happen?"

"Yep. I sure did," the farmer mumbles, unconcerned.

"Do you realize that was Air Force One, the airplane of the president of the United States?"

"Yep," the farmer replies, still unfazed.

"Were there any survivors?" the sheriff asks.

"Nope," the farmer replies, "they're all dead. I buried them all myself."

"President Obama is dead?" the sheriff asks with a lump in his throat.

"Well," the farmer grumbles, "he kept saying he wasn't but you know how much that guy lies!"

✱ GEORGE W. BUSH PASSES AWAY and finds himself in heaven. In an area reserved only for the most important of angels, he runs into Moses himself. Moses ignores the newest member of heaven. This agitates the former president. Bush approaches Moses in line for the grand buffet and says, "What gives, Moses? How come you won't say hello to me?" Moses looks at the former leader of the free world and explains, "Well the last time I talked to a Bush, my people ended up wandering the desert for forty years."

✱ "WHO SUCCEEDED THE FIRST PRESIDENT of the United States?" a teacher asks her class of students studying to become American citizens.

An older man in the back of the room raises his hand and answers, "The second one."

CHAPTER 7

Sports and Entertainment

The worlds of sports and celebrity provide a nice distraction from the dullness of daily life. Thankfully, both fields are filled with eccentric characters and personalities just slightly off center, which makes poking fun at them all the easier.

Music

* WHY DOES SNOOP DOGG CARRY an umbrella? Fo' drizzle.

* YESTERDAY I FOUND A JUSTIN Bieber concert ticket nailed to a tree, so I took it. You never know when you might need a nail.

* A MAN OPENED HIS FRIDGE and swore he heard two onions singing a Bee Gees song. After closer inspection, he realized it was just chives talking.

* HOW DO YOU WAKE LADY Gaga up from a nap? Poker face.

* IF GOD IS LOVE, AND love is blind, then doesn't that make Stevie Wonder God?

* KANYE WEST COMPARES HIMSELF TO Michelangelo, Picasso, Walt Disney, and Steve Jobs. Apparently none of them could sing, either.

✱ DID YOU KNOW DOLLY PARTON was once a schoolteacher? She loved the kids, but her biggest problem was after she wrote something on the blackboard, she'd turn around and accidentally wipe it off.

✱ HOW DID MICHAEL JACKSON PICK his nose? Usually from a catalog.

✱ A WOMAN IS READING THE newspaper while her husband is watching television next to her on the couch. Suddenly, she bursts out laughing.

"Listen to this story," she says. "A man put out a classified ad and he's offering to swap his wife for season tickets to the Red Sox."

"Wow," her husband says, not looking away from the television.

She begins to tease him and asks, "Would you swap me for season tickets?"

"Absolutely not," he answers without giving it a second thought.

"How sweet," she says, hugging him close.

"I mean," he continues, "the season is almost half over now."

✱ WHAT'S THE DIFFERENCE BETWEEN AN onion and an accordion? No one cries when you chop up an accordion.

✱ WHAT'S BEETHOVEN'S FAVORITE FRUIT? BA-NA-NA-NAAA!

✱ WHAT DO YOU GET WHEN you drop a piano down a mine shaft? A flat minor.

✱ HOW CAN YOU TELL THE difference between all the banjo songs? By their names.

✱ WHEN MOZART PASSED AWAY, HE was buried in a churchyard. A couple days later, the town drunk was walking through the cemetery and heard some strange noise coming from the area where Mozart was buried. Terrified, the drunk ran and got the town magistrate to come and listen to it. When the magistrate arrived, he bent his ear to the grave, listened for a moment, and said, "Ah, yes, that's Mozart's Ninth Symphony, being played backward."

He listened a while longer, and said, "There's the Eighth Symphony, and it's backward, too. Most puzzling."

So the magistrate kept listening. "There's the Seventh . . . the Sixth . . . the Fifth . . ." Suddenly the realization of what was happening dawned on the magistrate; he stood up and announced to the crowd that had gathered in the cemetery, "My fellow citizens, there's nothing to worry about. It's just Mozart decomposing."

✳ A PIANO TEACHER TURNS TO his student and says, "You should have taken up piano years ago."

"Why?" the student asks. "Is it because I've got a natural talent?"

"No," replies the teacher. "Because you would have given up by now."

✳ A WOMAN ANSWERS THE DOOR to find a man carrying a large box of tools.

"Can I help you?" the woman asks.

"Yes, I'm here to tune your piano," the man explains.

"I didn't call for a piano tuner," the woman replies.

"Yeah, I know," the man says. "Your neighbors sent me."

✳ A PATRON APPROACHED A BARTENDER and asked, "How late does the band usually play?" "Typically," the bartender replied, "about a half-beat behind the drummer."

✳ ISN'T IT IRONIC THAT PEOPLE born with clubbed feet are generally bad at dancing?

✳ WHAT HAPPENS IF YOU SING country music backward? You get your job and your wife back.

✳ A COWBOY AND A BIKER are on death row, and are to be executed on the same day. The day comes, and the warden asks the cowboy if he has a last request, to which the cowboy replies, "I sure do, Warden. I'd be mighty grateful if you'd play 'Achy Breaky Heart' for me before my time is up."

"Sure enough, cowboy, we can do that," says the warden.

He turns to the biker. "And you, biker, what's your last request?"

"My last request is that you kill me first."

✳ LITTLE NOAH COMES INTO THE house with a new harmonica. "Grandpa, do you mind if I play this in here?"

"Of course not, Noah. I love music. In fact, when your grandma and I were young, music saved my life."

"What happened?" asks Noah.

"Well, it was during the famous Johnstown flood. The dam broke and when the water hit our house it knocked it right off the foundation. Grandma got on the dining room table and floated out safely."

"How about you?"

"Me? I accompanied her on the piano!"

✳ A PIANO PLAYER GOES INTO a bar, but keeps fidgeting so much that he cannot enjoy his drink. Finally, the bartender asks him what is wrong. The piano player replies, "My keys, my keys! I can't seem to find my keys!"

Movies

✳ WHY DID THE MAN WATCH *Lord of the Rings* over and over again? Out of hobbit.

✳ DID YOU HEAR THE BAD news about the Sylvester Stallone marathon? It got off to a *Rocky* start.

✳ BUCKWHEAT OF THE LITTLE RASCALS fame grew up, became a Muslim, and changed his name. He now goes by Kareem of Wheat.

✳ "I THINK I FINALLY FIGURED out the ratings system," one movie usher says to the other during their shift. "Rated G means the hero gets the girl, PG means the villain gets the girl, and rated R means everybody gets the girl."

✳ A WOMAN IS EATING LUNCH at a Los Angeles restaurant when she bumps into her favorite movie star in the ladies' room. Constantly in trouble with drugs and the police, the star mentions to the fan that she is already writing her memoir. "Some of these stories are so crazy," she admits, "the publisher is considering holding the book until I pass away." "Wow," the fan replies, "so I guess it will be on shelves in a couple months?"

✳ A YOUNG ACTOR CALLS HIS agent from the set of his first film. He is playing the lead role for the first time in his career.

"How's it going?" the agent asks.

"It's amazing!" the actor gushes. "The director told me that my performance is making him consider making two films with me."

"Two?" the agent replies.

"Yeah," the actor says, "my first and my last."

✳ AT THE MOVIE THEATER, A girl returning to her seat taps the shoulder of the man in the last seat in the row.

"Excuse me," she says, "but did I step on your toe on the way to the bathroom?"

"As a matter of fact, you did," says the man, expecting an apology.

"Oh good," says the girl, "then this is my row."

Sports

✳ AFTER A DAY OF ENTERTAINING the troops, the Dallas Cowboys cheerleaders meet with the base commander to discuss the rest of the evening.

"Would you girls like to mess with the enlisted men or the officers this evening?" the commander asks.

"I don't think it matters to the ladies," the head cheerleader says, "but I'm sure a lot of the girls would like to get something to eat first."

✳ DID YOU HEAR ABOUT THE tragedy involving the U.S. Synchronized Swimming Team? The captain had a heart attack in the water and drowned and the rest of the team really didn't have a choice.

 Comedy Facts

The first comedian to win a Grammy award was Shelley Berman in 1959 for his album *Inside Shelley Berman*. Berman took home the award for Comedy Album/Spoken Word. Berman was also the first stand-up to perform at Carnegie Center.

✳ TWO FRIENDS ARE HAVING DRINKS and talking about their vivid dreams. "Last night," says the first man, "I dreamt I was playing a round of golf at Augusta. It was a gorgeous day and I was shooting the round of my life."

"That's amazing," the second man says. "Last night I dreamt I was in bed with two women."

"What!" his friend cries. "You had two women and you didn't even give your best friend a call?"

"I did," explains the second man, "but your wife told me you were out golfing."

✳ A RETIRED BOXER GOES TO see his doctor because he's having trouble sleeping. "Have you tried counting sheep?" the doctor asks.

"I tried," the boxer explains, "but every time I get to the number nine I stand up."

✳ A SOCCER HOOLIGAN APPEARS BEFORE a judge. He is charged with disorderly conduct and assault after a match. The arresting officer states that the accused had thrown something into the river not far from the stadium.

"What exactly did the accused throw into the river?" the judge asks.

"Stones, sir," the officer replies.

The judge is confused. "Well, that's hardly an offense, officer."

"It was in this case, sir," the officer explains. "Stones is the name of the referee."

✳ A FRANTIC FATHER CALLS THE family doctor on the phone. "Doc, you've got to come quick! My three-year-old son just swallowed all of my golf tees."

"All right, stay calm," the doctor tells the father. "I'll be over in ten minutes."

"What should I do in the meantime?" the father asks.

The doctor answers, "I guess you could practice your putting."

✳ A YOUNG MAN AND A priest are playing a round of golf together. At a short par-3 the priest asks the young man, "What are you going to use on this hole, my son?"

The young man answers, "I'm thinking an 8 iron, Father. How about you?"

The priest says, "I'm going to hit a soft 7 iron and pray."

The young man hits his 8 iron and puts the ball on the green. The priest taps his 7 iron and dribbles the ball out a good distance from the hole. As they get into their cart, the young man says to the priest, "I don't know about you, Father, but in my church, when we pray, we keep our heads down."

 Ask the Comedian

How does a person get into stand-up?
There really is no specific course of action to performing stand-up, but there is one thing every comic does at the start of his or her career—get in front of an audience as often as possible. Take advantage of open mic nights, community gatherings, or anywhere there is a stage and an audience willing to listen to people perform. Go to as many of these events as you can and work on your material. Eventually, you'll have a set of material (at least ten minutes) with which to approach the people who book comedy clubs.

✳ TODD TOOK A WEEK OFF from the office. He booked a vacation to go skiing. Before his first trip down the mountain, he heard an unbelievable rumble, and before he could move he was covered in snow. He found shelter in a small cave and was able to start a fire and make himself comfortable until help arrived. After a few hours, there was a digging at the front of the cave.

"Who's there?" Todd called out from inside the cave.

"Hello!" a voice called. "It's the Red Cross!"

"Beat it!" Todd yelled back. "I already donated twice this year."

✳ THE OWNER OF A RACEHORSE is angry because the horse he paid so much money for has yet to win a race.

"Listen to me," the man says, grabbing the horse by the harness. "You'd better win this race or you'll be working the farm tomorrow."

The horses line up in the gates, the starting gun sounds, and the gate is removed. All of the horses take off for the finish line, except the owner's horse. He is fast asleep in his starting pen.

"What the heck do you think you're doing?" the owner yells at the horse.

"I'm grabbing some rest," says the horse. "I've got to work the farm early tomorrow morning."

✳ WHAT TIME DOES SERENA WILLIAMS go to bed? Tennish.

✳ GIVE A MAN A FISH and he will eat for a day. Teach him how to fish and he will sit in a boat and drink beer all day.

✳ A GOALKEEPER HOSTED A CELEBRATORY dinner at his house after his team won the league championship. Before dinner, he asked the coach to say grace. The coach concluded his prayer by saying, "We ask that you bless this food in the name of the father, and of the son, and of the goalie host."

✳ OLD MAN MORTY IS TELLING his grandson about his days as a prize fighter. "Then there was the match against Hammerhands

Callahan," Morty begins. "It was quite a bout. By the third round, I had him nervous."

"Really?" his grandson asks excitedly.

"Yup," Morty replies, "he was pretty nervous he was going to kill me."

✴ A GROUP OF CHESS ENTHUSIASTS check into a hotel and are standing in the lobby discussing their recent tournament victories. After about an hour, the manager comes out of the office and asks them to disperse.

"But why?" they ask, as they move off.

"Because," he says, "I can't stand chess nuts boasting in an open foyer."

✴ THE HARDEST PART ABOUT WATER polo is keeping the horse from drowning.

✴ FOOTBALL IS A GAME PLAYED by incredibly fit men who run around for three hours for the amusement of millions of out-of-shape fans.

✴ WHILE SITTING ON THE DECK of the course bar after a round of golf, Bill is hit in the head with an errant drive. By the time the offending golfer finds him, Bill is already angry and holding an ice pack to his head.

"I'm so sorry!" the golfer says. "It just got away from me!"

"You'll be more than sorry!" Bill yells. "I'm going to sue you for $5 million for your carelessness."

"I yelled 'fore,'" the golfer explains.

"Fine," Bill answers. "I'll take four."

✴ NEGOTIATIONS BETWEEN UNION MEMBERS AND their employer are at an impasse. The union denies that the workers are flagrantly abusing the sick-leave provisions set out by their contract. One morning at the bargaining table, the company's chief negotiator holds the morning edition of the newspaper.

"This man," he announces, "called in sick yesterday!" There on the sports page was a photo of the supposedly ill employee, who had just won a local golf tournament with an excellent score. A union negotiator breaks the silence in the room.

"Wow!" he says. "Just think of the score he could have had if he hadn't been sick!"

 Famous Funnies

> "If a woman has to choose between catching a fly ball and saving an infant's life, she will choose to save the infant's life without even considering if there is a man on base."—Dave Barry

✳ A SKYDIVING STUDENT IS BEING instructed on how to open his chute. "You count to ten out loud," the instructor says, "and then pull the rip cord." The student asks, "W-w-w-w-w-h-h-a-t w-w-w-w-w-a-s that that that num-num-number a-a-a-gain?"

The instructor replies, "Two."

✳ THE OLYMPICS THIS YEAR FEATURED a representative from each of two hundred different countries. One more representative and they'll match the number in the Pitt-Jolie family.

✳ A GOLFER SETS HIS BALL on the tee and lines up his shot. He takes a massive swing and puts the ball into a huge forest of trees along the fairway. He finds his ball and sees an opening he thinks he could sneak the ball through. Taking out his 3 wood, the golfer takes another mighty swing. The ball bounces off a tree and fires back at him, nailing him in the forehead and killing him instantly. St. Peter meets him at the pearly gates and asks how his golf game had been progressing.

The golfer says to St. Peter confidently, "Got up here in two, didn't I?"

✻ TWO GOLFERS ARE STARTING A round. "That's a weird-looking ball you're using. What kind is it?"

"Oh, it's awesome," the second golfer exclaims. "It's a completely unlosable ball! If it goes into the bushes, the ball lights up. If it lands in a water hazard, it floats to the surface. If it's dark out, it emits a beeping sound until you find it. The ball is sensational."

"Wow, that's amazing," says the first golfer. "Where did you get it?"

"Last time I golfed," reveals the second golfer, "I found it in the woods."

✻ A LOCAL BAR WAS SO sure that its bartender was the strongest man around that it had a standing $10,000 bet with patrons. The bartender would squeeze a lemon until all the juice ran into a glass, and hand the lemon to a patron. Anyone who could squeeze out one more drop of juice would win the money. Many people had tried over time but nobody could do it. One day, a scrawny little man comes in wearing thick glasses.

"I'd like to try the bet," he says in a tiny, squeaky voice. After the laughter has died down, the bartender grabs a lemon and squeezes away. He hands the wrinkled remains of the rind to the little man. But the crowd's laughter turns to total silence as the man clenches his fist around the lemon and six drops fall into the glass. As the crowd cheers, the bartender pays the $10,000 and asks the little man what he does for a living.

"Are you a lumberjack or a weightlifter, or what?"

"I work for the Internal Revenue Service."

✻ AN OLD MAN AND HIS wife are in bed. After lying silently for a few minutes, the old man farts and says, "Seven points."

His wife rolls over and says, "What in the heck are you talking about?"

The old man answers, "I'm playing fart football!"

A few minutes later the wife farts and says, "Touchdown! Tie score."

After about five minutes the old man farts again and says, "Touchdown! I'm winning 14 to 7!"

Furious about losing, the wife rips another fart and yells out, "The score is tied!"

The pressure is on and the old man refuses to lose. He strains incredibly hard but instead of farting he accidentally poops the bed. The wife hears the noise and asks, "What in the world was that noise?"

The old man replies, "That's the whistle for halftime. Switch sides."

＊ TWO MEN GO HUNTING IN the forest. They are walking along with their guns and enjoying the outdoors when one man suddenly collapses. His friend grabs him to see what's wrong, but he won't move. He knows something is wrong and calls 911. The man shouts frantically into the phone, "My buddy just collapsed! He isn't moving and I think he's dead! What do I do?"

"Well first," the 911 operator replies calmly, "you need to make sure he is actually dead."

The operator hears the man leave the phone for a moment. She hears footsteps followed by a moment of silence and then a loud bang.

The friend returns to the phone. "Okay, he's dead, now what?"

＊ A COUPLE WERE GOLFING ONE day on a very exclusive golf course lined with million-dollar houses. On the third tee, the husband said, "Honey, be very careful when you drive the ball. Don't knock out any windows. It will cost us a fortune to fix."

The wife teed up and shanked it right through the window of the biggest house on the course.

The husband cringed and said, "I told you to watch out for the houses. All right, let's go up there, apologize, and see how much it's going to cost us."

They walked up, knocked on the door, and heard a voice say, "Come on in."

When they opened the door they saw glass all over the place and a broken bottle lying on its side in the foyer.

A man on the couch said, "Are you the people who broke the window?"

"Uh yeah, sorry about that," the husband replied.

"No, actually I want to thank you. I am a genie who was trapped for a thousand years in that bottle. You have released me. I am allowed to grant three wishes. I will give you each one wish, and I will keep the last one for myself," the genie said.

"Okay," the husband said. "I want a million dollars a year for the rest of my life."

"No problem—it's the least I can do. And you, what do you want?" the genie asked the wife.

"I want a house in every country of the world," she said.

"Consider it done," the genie said.

"And what is your wish, genie?" the husband asked.

"Well, since I have not had love with a woman in a thousand years, my wish is to sleep with your wife."

The husband looked at the wife and said, "Well, we did get a lot of money and all those houses, honey. I guess I wouldn't mind."

The genie took the wife upstairs and ravished her for two hours. After it was all over, the genie rolled over, looked at the wife, and said, "How old is your husband anyway?" "Thirty-five," she said.

"Really? And he still believes in genies?"

✱ A FISHERMAN SITS ANGRILY IN his small boat. He hasn't caught a thing all morning. Suddenly, another man in the boat across from him opens his tackle box, removes a small compact mirror, and begins to shine it into the water.

"What are you doing?" the first man asks.

"This is how I catch fish. The shiny light attracts the fish, they come close to the surface to see what's going on, and I grab them with my net."

"Does that really work?"

"Every time," the man proclaims.

After a moment of thought, the first fisherman says, "I'll give you fifty dollars for that mirror." The second fisherman agrees. After a few minutes of shining the light onto the water, the first fisherman asks, "By the way, how many fish have you caught this week?"

The second fisherman smiles and replies, "Actually, you're the sixth."

 Comedy Facts

Eddie Murphy's live comedy movie *Raw* debuted in theaters on December 18, 1987. The movie made over $9 million in its opening weekend and grossed over $50 million over its entire theater run. It is still the highest-earning comedy concert movie of all time.

✳ A GOLFER IS HAVING A horrible day on the course. After another shot into the woods, he says aloud, "I'd move heaven and earth to break 100 on this course."

His caddy puts the club back into his bag and says, "Try just heaven, because you've already moved most of the earth."

✳ A SAN FRANCISCO GIANTS FAN, a San Diego Padres fan, and a Los Angeles Dodgers fan are climbing a mountain and arguing about which one loves his team more. The Padres fan insists he's the most loyal.

"This is for San Diego!" he yells, and jumps off the side of the mountain. Not to be outdone, the Giants fan is next to profess his love for his team.

He yells, "This is for San Francisco!" and pushes the Dodgers fan off the mountain.

✳ TWO GUYS ARE PLAYING GOLF. Two women in front of them are really taking their time and are slowing the men up.

One man says to his friend, "I'm gonna go ask those ladies if we can play through."

He starts walking, but about halfway there, he turns around. When he gets back, his friend asks what happened.

He replies, "One of those women is my wife, and the other is my mistress. Will *you* go talk to them?"

So the second man starts to walk over. He gets halfway there and turns around. When he gets back, his friend asks, "Now what happened?"

To this he replies, "Small world."

✱ A ROOKIE PITCHER IS STRUGGLING on the mound, so the catcher walks up to have a quick talk with him.

"I think I've figured out your problem," the catcher tells the shaky southpaw. "You always lose control at exactly the same point in every game."

The pitcher feels a little relieved, thinking he has the answer to his issue.

"When do I usually lose my control?" he asks his battery mate.

"It's usually," the catcher admits, "right after the National Anthem."

✱ TWO OLD MEN ARE IN the middle of an intense chess match. In the middle of player one's next move, player two lets out a loud sneeze.

"God bless you," player one says.

Player two snaps back, "Did you come here to talk or did you come here to play?"

Comedy Facts

While there are countless comedy festivals and events around the world during the calendar year, here are three of the most influential and popular: the Edinburgh Festival Fringe in Edinburgh, Scotland; the Just for Laughs festival in Montreal, Canada; and the Melbourne International Comedy Festival in Melbourne, Australia.

✳ A SKYDIVING INSTRUCTOR IS ANSWERING questions for his beginner's class.

"So if my parachute doesn't open," a student asks, "and my reserve chute doesn't work, how long have I got until I hit the ground?"

The instructor tells the man, "You've got the rest of your life."

Miscellaneous

✳ AFTER YEARS OF GAMBLING, AN unlucky gambler finally figures out the way to leave Las Vegas with a small fortune. He goes to Las Vegas with a large fortune.

✳ TOM AND CLARK ARE STANDING on the roof of their building drinking a few beers on their break when Clark says, "Hey Tom, did you know that if you jump off this building, after you get down so far, a draft will pull you back inside the building on the third floor?"

"Get outta here," says Tom.

"I'm serious. Watch me," Clark says. Clark hops off the building and sure enough, he is taken in by the draft to the third-floor window. He takes the elevator back to the top and Tom is standing there in awe.

"I can't believe it," says Tom.

"I know. You should try it."

So Tom hops off and plunges into the ground.

A doorman working below sees Tom splat to the ground and screams back up, "Superman, you're a real jerk when you're drunk."

✳ WHAT DO YOU CALL A person who pretends to be a college student? A college athlete.

 Famous Funnies

"Burt Reynolds once asked me out. I was in his room."—Phyllis Diller

✳ A MAN IS DOING THE morning crossword puzzle on his commute into work. An elderly nun in the seat next to his is doing the same puzzle. She notices and asks for his assistance. "Excuse me, son," the nun says, "but did you happen to get the answer for 42 down?"

The man looks down at his puzzle and replies, "A four-letter word for 'intercourse' and the last letter is K. Yes, it's 'talk.'"

✳ WHY DON'T BATMAN AND ROBIN go fishing anymore? Robin always eats the worms.

✳ HOW DO YOU FIND RONALD McDonald at a nude beach? You look for the sesame seed buns!

✳ DID YOU HEAR OJ SIMPSON is doing stand-up in jail? He kills.

✳ SHERLOCK HOLMES AND DR. WATSON go on a camping trip. After a good meal and a bottle of wine, they lie down for the night and go to sleep. Some hours later, Holmes awakens and nudges his faithful friend. "Watson, look up at the sky and tell me what you see."

Watson replies, "I see millions and millions of stars."

"What does that tell you?" Watson ponders for a minute.

"Astronomically, it tells me that there are millions of galaxies, and potentially billions of planets. Astrologically, I observe that

Saturn is in Leo. Horologically, I deduce that the time is approximately a quarter past three. Theologically, I can see that God is all-powerful and that we are small and insignificant. Meteorologically, I suspect that we will have a beautiful day tomorrow. What does it tell you?"

Holmes is silent for a minute, then says, "It tells me that someone has stolen our tent."

＊ STRIP POKER IS THE ONLY game where the more you lose, the more you have to show for it.

 ## Famous Funnies

"Anyone who's just driven 90 yards against huge men trying to kill them has earned the right to do Jazz hands."—Craig Ferguson

＊ DAVID HASSELHOFF WALKS INTO A bar and orders a beer. The bartender says, "You've got it, Mr. Hasselhoff."

Hasselhoff replies, "Thanks, but you can just call me 'The Hoff.'"

"Sure thing," says the bartender. "No hassel."

＊ PRINCE CHARLES VISITED IRAN ON a peacekeeping mission. He asked the president of Iran, "Where is the Shah?"

The president was puzzled. "The Shah?" he replied. "There is no Shah. We removed the Shah years ago."

"Very well," said Charles, "well, I suppose I'll just have to settle for a bath."

＊ A WOMAN CALLED QVC LATE one night. A customer service rep answered and asked, "Would you like to purchase something tonight?" The woman responded, "No thanks, I'm just browsing."

✱ DONALD TRUMP DOES A GREAT deal for the less fortunate. For example, he allows a blind man to cut his hair.

✱ HOW MANY MAGICIANS DOES IT take to change a light bulb? Into what?

 Famous Funnies

"I saw on the news that Lindsay Lohan was busted for having coke in the car. That's a story? Call me when they find a book in the car."
—Dave Attell

✱ A MAN VISITS THE ER with blood trickling down his face. The doctor on duty asks how he got the giant gash in his forehead. "I was riding the roller coaster at the amusement park. As we came up to the top of the highest loop, I noticed a little sign by the side of the track. I tried to read it but it was very small and I couldn't make it out. I was so curious that I decided to ride the coaster again, but we went by so quickly that I couldn't see what the sign said. By now, I was determined to read that sign so I got on a third time. As we reached the top, I stood up in the car to get a better view."

"And did you manage to see what the sign said that time?" asks the doctor.

"Yes."

"What did it say?"

"It said, 'Please don't stand up in the car!'"

CHAPTER 8

Health, Aging, and Dying

There's an old saying that there are two things no one can avoid: death and taxes. While you might be able to avoid taxes for a while, there is no cheating death. It's inevitable. Luckily, old age and its ailments will make a person either forget death is coming or wish it got there sooner. In any event, these jokes prove that laughter is the best medicine.

Doctor Visits

✳ A MAN GOES TO A doctor for his yearly routine physical. The nurse starts with the basic health questions.

"How much do you weigh?" she asks.

"Oh, about 165 pounds," he says.

The nurse puts him on the scale and his actual weight is 187.

The nurse then asks, "And how tall are you?"

"Oh, about six feet tall," he says. The nurse checks and sees that he's only five foot eight. She then takes his blood pressure and tells him it's incredibly high.

"High!" the man exclaims. "Well, what do you expect? When I came in here today I was tall and lanky. Now I'm short and fat!"

✳ A MAN WITH A BROKEN hand says to the doctor, "Will I be able to play guitar after the operation on my hand?"

The doctor says, "Yes, of course."

"That's great!" says the man. "I never could before."

✳ A WOMAN EXPLAINS TO HER doctor her recent issues with going to the bathroom.

"I've had horrible constipation," she explains. "I haven't been able to go for weeks."

"Are you doing anything for it?" the doctor asks.

"Well, I'll force myself to sit on the toilet for a half hour in the morning and a half hour before bed."

"No, I meant are you taking anything?"

"Oh," she replies. "Yeah, I usually take a magazine."

✳ A MAN VISITS THE DOCTOR with a head of lettuce sticking out of his ear. The doctor says, "Well I can see your issue right off the bat, Mr. Timmins."

The man replies, "This is just the tip of the iceberg, doc."

 Comedy Facts

In the 1980s, Comic Relief was born in the United Kingdom. Comic Relief is a charity organization that raises money for the homeless through comedy benefits. The American version of Comic Relief was founded in 1986 by Bob Zmuda, the former co-conspirator of Andy Kaufman. The event was aired on HBO each year. The first special was hosted by Billy Crystal, Robin Williams, and Whoopi Goldberg.

✳ A MAN VISITS THE DOCTOR for a routine checkup. The doctor tells him he has to undergo surgery.

"What are you operating for?" the man asks.

"For $10,000," the doctor replies.

"No," says the man. "I meant, what's the reason?"

The doctor responds, "I told you, for $10,000."

✳ A MAN GOES TO THE doctor with a long history of migraine headaches. When the doctor does his history and physical, he discovers that the poor guy has tried practically every therapy known to man for his migraines, with no improvement.

"Listen," says the doctor. "I have migraines too and the advice I'm going to give you isn't really anything I learned in medical school, but it's advice that I've gotten from my own experience. When I have a migraine, I go home, get in a nice hot bathtub, and soak for a while. Then I have my wife sponge me off with the hottest water I can stand, especially around the forehead. This helps a little. Then I get out of the tub, take her into the bedroom, and even if my head is killing me, I force myself to make love to her. Almost always, the headache is immediately gone. Now, give it a try, and come back and see me in six weeks."

Six weeks later, the patient returns with a big grin.

"Doc! I took your advice and it works! It really works! I've had migraines for seventeen years and this is the first time anyone has ever helped me!"

"Well," says the physician, "I'm glad I could help."

"By the way, Doc," the patient adds, "you have a really nice house!"

✳ A MAN ASKS HIS GOOD friend if he can recommend a doctor. "Yeah," the man says, "I'll give you the number to the guy we go see. He's a family doctor. He treats mine and I support his."

✳ A MAN WENT TO THE dentist to have a cavity worked on. The dentist was on vacation so the man settled for the doctor filling in.

✳ A WOMAN RUNS INTO A doctor's office and says, "Doctor! You have to help me! Everywhere I touch on my body it hurts!"

The doctor replies, "Show me." So the woman pokes her ankle and screams in pain. She pokes her knee and yells again. She pokes her forehead and screams louder than before. She is about to continue when the doctor says, "That's enough, let me think this over." He thinks for a minute and says, "I think I know what your problem is. You broke your finger."

✸ A WORRIED FATHER CALLS THE family doctor because he thinks his teen son has caught a venereal disease.

"I think he got it from the maid," says the concerned dad, "and I've also been sleeping with the maid."

"Okay," the doctor replies calmly. "Well, when you bring him into the office we'll take a look at you as well."

"And that's not all," the father continues. "I think I might have given it to his mother."

"Oh no!" cries the doctor, "well, now we might all have it!"

✸ A DOCTOR TELLS HIS PATIENT he's got six months to live.

"Is there anything I can do?" the man asks. "Well, you could take a ton of mud baths," the doctor tells the dying patient.

"Do you think that will cure me?" the patient asks optimistically. "No," the doctor replies, "but it will get you accustomed to lying in dirt."

 ## Ask the Comedian

Are there any topics that are off limits?
With comedy, there are really no topics off limits, but there are several topics a person should avoid. It's usually best to stay away from religion, politics, or personal or public tragedies that some might consider "too soon" to joke about. It also depends on the audience. It's always best to work as clean as possible. It avoids any possible issues.

✸ "I'M FEELING AWFUL," A MAN tells his doctor during a sick visit. "I think it might be my diet."

"Well, what are you eating every day?" the doctor asks while looking over the man's chart.

"Pool balls," the man answers.

"Excuse me?" the doctor replies with a confused expression.

"Pool balls. I eat two reds in the morning. Three blue for lunch. A couple yellow for dinner, and the eight ball if I need a snack."

"Well I think I see your issue," the doctor tells the man. "You're not eating any greens."

✳ A WOMAN VISITED THE DOCTOR. She was waking up every morning feeling awful and only felt better after throwing up.

"Well, Mrs. Douglas," the doctor said, "I've got some good news for you."

"It's Miss Douglas," she corrected the doctor. "I'm single."

"Oh," said the doctor, "well, then maybe this news isn't so good."

✳ A SICK MAN GOES TO the doctor to get a better idea of what's wrong with him.

"Do you drink to excess?" the doctor asks the man.

"I'll pretty much drink to anything," the man replies.

✳ A GUY IS GOING ON an ocean cruise and he tells his doctor that he's worried about getting seasick. The doctor suggests, "Eat two pounds of stewed tomatoes before you leave the dock."

The guy replies, "Will that keep me from getting sick, Doc?"

The doctor says, "No, but it'll look really pretty in the water."

✳ A MAN GOES TO THE doctor and tells him, "Every morning, I wake up and look at my face in the morning and it makes me want to vomit. What's wrong with me?"

The doctor answers, "I'm not quite sure, but we can say that your eyesight is perfect."

✳ A MAN VISITS THE DOCTOR because he's suffering from a miserable winter cold. His doctor prescribes some antibiotics, but they don't help. On his next visit, the doctor gives the man a shot, but it doesn't do any good. On his third visit, the doctor tells the man to go home and take a steaming hot bath. As soon as he gets out of the bath, he should open all of the windows in his house and stand naked in the draft.

"But doctor," the man protests, "if I do that, I'll probably get pneumonia."

"I know," says the doctor. "But at least I know how to cure pneumonia."

 ## Joke Essentials

"People are saying that I'm an alcoholic, and that's not true, because I only drink when I work, and I'm a workaholic."—Ron White

✴ A WOMAN ACCOMPANIES HER HUSBAND to a doctor's visit. After the checkup, the doctor calls only her into his office. "The outlook isn't good," he tells her.

"Your husband is under a tremendous amount of stress. If you don't do exactly what I tell you, he may not survive to see the end of the month. Each morning, make him a nice healthy breakfast. Do the same for lunch and dinner. Always be in a pleasant mood around him and keep his spirits up. Don't burden him with chores or stress him with the details of your day. At night, if he's up for it, agree to any request for sexual pleasure. If you do all those things, he'll live a long life." On the way home, the husband asks his wife what the doctor said to her in the closed-door meeting.

She replies, "You're going to die."

✴ A MAN GOES TO THE dentist for his six-month exam. The man tells the dentist, "My teeth are great. I never use mouthwash, rarely brush my teeth, never floss, never use a breath mint, and eat onions and garlic with just about every meal. I also never have bad breath." The dentist agrees his teeth are decent but he will need an operation.

"On what?" the man asks.

The dentist responds quickly, "Your nose."

Hospitals

✳ TWO MEN ARE ROOMMATES IN a hospital. Because they are both weak from sickness, the men are unable to speak for weeks. Finally, one man says to the other, "American."

His roommate replies, "Canadian."

Another week goes by and the first man says weakly, "Danny." The roommate can only reply, "Phil."

Another week passes and the first man mutters to his roommate, "Cancer." His roommate replies back, "Virgo."

 Famous Funnies

> "Everything that used to be a sin is now a disease."—Bill Maher

✳ DID YOU HEAR ABOUT THE man who showed up in the ER covered in wood and hay with a toy horse lodged up his backside? He's in stable condition.

✳ A WOMAN VISITS A FRIEND in the hospital. She luckily hasn't been to a hospital in years so she is ignorant of most of the new technology. On the way up to her friend's room, the elevator doors open and a man pushing a massive machine gets onto the elevator.

"My God," the woman says, "I'd hate to be the person who gets hooked up to that machine."

"Me too," says the man, "because it's used to wax the floors."

✳ A GUY WALKS INTO A bathroom, sits down, and notices three buttons in front of him marked, WW, WA, and ATR. Curiosity gets the better of him so he decides to press WW. Suddenly, warm water sprays up his rear.

"Mmmm," he says to himself. "That was good."

So he presses WA and a jet of warm air dries his backside.

"Mmmm. Nice!"

So finally he can't resist pressing the ATR button. The next thing he knows, he is waking up in a hospital ward just as the nurse is entering the room.

"Nurse, Nurse! Where am I? What happened?"

The nurse replies, "You pressed the ATR button."

"What does ATR mean exactly?" asks the guy. The nurse replies, "Automatic tampon remover."

＊ AN ELDERLY MAN, ALREADY DRESSED and sitting on his hospital bed with a suitcase at his feet, insisted to the nurse that he didn't need help leaving the hospital. "I'm sorry, sir," the nurse said, "but hospital regulations require a wheelchair for all patients being discharged." After a chat about rules being rules, the man reluctantly let the nurse wheel him to the elevator. On the way down, the nurse asked him if his wife was going to meet him in the lobby.

"I don't know," the man replied, "she's still upstairs in the bathroom changing out of her hospital gown."

＊ A DOCTOR VISITS THE HOSPITAL room of an incredibly sick young man.

"I've got good news and bad news," the doctor starts.

"Wait," says the sick man. "Start with the bad news."

"The bad news is I've got to amputate both of your arms."

"Oh my God," the man cries. "What's the good news?"

"The good news is I'm willing to give you at least $200 for your watch," says the doctor.

Mental Health

＊ A DOCTOR WALKS INTO A room full of patients at a mental institution, takes out a pen, and draws a door on the wall. He then tells all the patients that whoever wants to escape should use that door. Immediately they all rush toward it, but of course cannot go through. However, one patient sits still in the back with a smile on his face. He has not moved at all. The doctor thinks he must be cured. He then asks the patient why he did not rush to the door, and the patient whispers, "They don't know that I'm the one who has the key."

✱ A PSYCHIATRIST IS EXPLAINING TO a patient that he's using alcohol as a crutch in life. "That can't be true," the man says. "If it's a crutch, why am I constantly falling-down drunk?"

✱ A PSYCHIATRIST IS MEETING WITH a patient for the first time. He's reviewing his paperwork and comments, "It says here you believe in reincarnation. How long have you believed that?"

The man thinks for a moment and replies, "Probably since I was a puppy."

✱ A MAN SEES A PSYCHIATRIST for the first time.

"What seems to be the main issue?" the psychiatrist asks.

"I don't think there is anything wrong with me," the man says, "but my wife sent me here because I like pancakes."

The psychiatrist responds, "Liking pancakes doesn't make you crazy. I like pancakes too."

"Great!" the man exclaims. "You should stop by my house. I've got a whole basement full of pancakes!"

✱ "HOW WAS YOUR PSYCHIATRIST APPOINTMENT?" one roommate asks the other.

"My therapist says I have a preoccupation with vengeance," the second roommate says. "We'll see about that."

✱ A DEPRESSED MAN GOES TO the library to find a research book on suicide.

"Where are your books on suicide?" he asks the librarian behind the help desk.

"Oh, those are in the fourth row on the left. Bottom shelf."

The man heads over to the section but finds the shelves empty. He returns to the help desk and explains the issue to the librarian.

"Yeah, that makes sense," she admits. "Those books get checked out but don't often get returned."

✳ A PATIENT AND PSYCHOLOGIST ARE meeting for the first time.

"I think I'm a goat," the patient tells the new doctor.

"All right," the doctor says as he jots notes down. "And how long have you had this feeling?"

The man tells him, "Ever since I was a kid."

✳ A PATIENT IN A MENTAL hospital would spend his entire day with his ear pressed up against a wall. The doctor would watch this man, day after day, sit against the wall. The doctor finally decides to see what the patient is always listening to, so he puts his ear up to the wall, and listens alongside the man. He hears nothing.

He turns to the mental patient and says, "I don't hear anything coming from the wall."

The mental patient replies, "Yeah, I know, and it's been like that for months!"

✳ A NEW PATIENT SETTLES COMFORTABLY onto the couch and the psychiatrist began his therapy session.

"I'm not aware of your exact problem," the doctor says, "so perhaps you should start at the very beginning."

"Of course," replies the patient. "In the beginning, I created the Heavens and the Earth . . ."

Getting Older

✳ A WOMAN GOES TO THE DMV to get her license renewed. She goes to pick up her new license at the front desk and cringes when she sees her new photo.

"Ugh," she says aloud at her face in the photo.

"What's wrong?" asks the clerk.

"I look so old in this photo."

The DMV clerk laughs and says, "Yeah, but think about how much you'll love it in five years when you come back to take another."

✱ THREE OLDER LADIES ARE DISCUSSING the trials of getting older. One says, "Sometimes I catch myself with a jar of mayonnaise in my hand in front of the refrigerator and can't remember whether I need to put it away or start making a sandwich."

The second lady chimes in, "Yes, sometimes I find myself on the landing of the stairs and can't remember whether I was on my way up or on my way down."

The third one responds, "Well, I'm sure glad I don't have that problem, knock on wood." She raps her knuckles on the table, then says, "That must be the door, I'll get it."

✱ TWO MEN ARE SITTING IN a bar drinking. The first man notices two old men across the bar. He points at them and says to his friend, "That's us in about ten years."

His friend looks up, laughs, puts his head back down, and says, "That's us now, because that's a mirror."

 Famous Funnies

"You know what the DMV should do? When you walk in the door, they should have somebody hiding just punch you in the face. Because at least after, you can be like, 'Ah! All right, well, waiting in line's not so bad after the punch in the face!'"—Dane Cook

✱ A MIDDLE-AGED MAN GOES TO the doctor about his recent issues with memory loss. "Doctor, I just can't seem to remember much anymore."

"Okay," the doctor says sympathetically, "it might be an issue we can get a grip on. When exactly did you begin having this issue?"

The man looks at the doctor and replies, "What issue?"

✱ A WOMAN BUYS HERSELF A facelift for her birthday. She spends $5,000 and feels pretty good about the results. One week later, on her way home she stops at a newsstand to buy a paper. Before leaving, she asks the sales clerk, "I hope you don't mind my asking, but how old do you think I am?"

"About thirty-two," the clerk replies.

"I'm actually forty-seven," the woman says happily. A little while later, she goes into McDonald's and, upon getting her order, asks the counter girl the same question.

The girl replies, "I'd guess about twenty-nine."

The woman replies, "Nope, I am forty-seven."

Now she is feeling really good about herself. While waiting for the bus home, she asks an old man the same question.

He replies, "I'm seventy-eight and my eyesight is starting to go. Although, when I was young, there was a sure way to tell how old a woman was, but it requires you to let me put my hands up your shirt and feel your boobs. Then I can tell exactly how old you are." They wait in silence on the empty street until curiosity gets the best of the woman, and she finally says, "What the hell, go ahead."

The old man slips both hands up her shirt, under her bra, and begins to feel around. After a couple of minutes, she says, "Okay, okay, how old am I?"

He removes his hands and says, "You are forty-seven."

Stunned, the woman says, "That is amazing! How did you know?"

The old man replies, "I was behind you in line at McDonald's."

✱ A MAN IS STANDING ON the scale in his bathroom and sucking in his gut. His wife catches him and says, "That's not going to help at all."

"Yes it is," the man barks. "Now I can see the numbers!"

Old Age

* TWO OLD MEN ARE SITTING on a park bench. The first man takes a look into his friend's ear and says, "Do you know you've got a suppository stuck in your ear?"

"Really?" says the first man. "I had no idea. But I guess that explains where I put my hearing aid."

* "MY GRANDMOTHER HAS ALZHEIMER'S," A teen tells his friend as they walk past her sitting in the living room.

"That sucks," the friend says.

"Yeah, but it's got some upside," the teen replies. "Like when I get twenty dollars for my birthday every week."

* TWO OLD WOMEN ARE DISCUSSING the disgusting habits of their husbands. "Even after all these years, my husband will not stop biting his nails," the first woman explains.

"My husband had the same habit," the second woman explains, "but I fixed that. I just hid his teeth."

* A GRANDFATHER IS WALKING HOME with his granddaughter after church. "Did God make you, PopPop?" the girl asks.

"Yep! He certainly did," the old man answers.

"And did he make me too?" she asks next.

"Of course he did," the old man answers again.

"Well," she replies, "he's certainly getting better at it."

* "DO YOU REALIZE YOU WERE speeding?" the officer asks the old woman after pulling her over.

"Yes, officer," she replies, embarrassed, "but I've got a very good excuse."

"What's that?" he asks.

"I'm trying to get where I'm going before I forget where I'm going."

✳ AN OLD WOMAN ACCIDENTALLY DROPS her fake teeth at the park while walking her dog. She can't find the teeth anywhere in the tall grass. A man spots her bending over and asks what she lost. "I dropped my false teeth somewhere around here."

"Oh," the man says, "that's no big deal. Here, try this pair on."

He hands her a set of teeth that are too big for her mouth. He hands her a second set of teeth that are too small. Finally, the third set fits just right.

"Thank you so much," the old woman says. "Do you have a business card? I've been looking for a good dentist for some time."

"Oh, I'm not a dentist," the man replies. "I'm an undertaker."

✳ AN OLD COUPLE ARE SITTING in their living room. The old woman leans over and says to the old man, "Remember when we were younger and you used to hold my hand?" The old man grabs the old woman's hand.

Then she says, "Remember when we were younger and you used to put your arm around me?" The old man puts his arm around the old woman.

Then she says, "Remember when we were younger and you used to nibble on my ear?" To the old woman's surprise, the old man gets up off the couch and starts to walk away.

"Honey, where are you going?" she asks. The old man replies, "I'm going to get my dentures."

✳ THREE OLD MEN ARE TAKING a memory test at the nursing home. The doctor asks the first man, "What's four times four?"

"Two-thousand and seven," the first man answers.

The doctor turns to the next man and asks the same question, "What is four times four?" The second man answers, "Tuesday."

The doctor turns to the third man and again asks, "What's four times four?"

The man looks at him and says, "Sixteen."

"That's correct," the doctor says. "And how did you get to that number?"

"Simple," the old man replies, "I just subtracted two-thousand and seven from Tuesday."

✳ AN OLD MAN ENTERS A confessional and proudly exclaims, "Father, I have to tell you what happened to me last night. I'm ninety years old, and I made love to two eighteen-year-old women for eight hours!"

The stern priest replies, "That is a sin. I will have to give you a penance."

"Father, you can't give me a penance."

"Why not?" the priest asks.

"Because I'm Jewish," the man responds.

The priest is confused and asks, "Then why are you telling me?"

The old man responds excitedly, "I'm telling everyone!"

 Famous Funnies

"If you're older, you're smarter. I just believe that. If you're in an argument with someone older than you, you should listen to them. Even if they're wrong, their wrongness is rooted in more information than you have."—Louis CK

✳ A NEW MAN IS BROUGHT into a prison cell with a cellmate who is already 100 years old. The new cellmate asks the old man his story. The old con says, "You look at me, I'm old and worn out, but if you can believe it, I used to live the life of Riley. I wintered on the Riviera, had a boat, four luxury cars, dated the most beautiful women, and I ate in all the best restaurants around the world."

The new man asks, "What happened?"

"Riley finally realized his credit cards were missing."

✳ A SENIOR CITIZEN SAYS TO his eighty year-old buddy: "So I hear you're getting married?"

"Yep!"

"Do I know her?"

"Nope!"

"This woman, is she good-looking?"

"Not really."

"Is she a good cook?"

"Naw, she can't cook too well."

"Does she have lots of money?"

"Nope! Poor as a church mouse."

"Well, then, is she good in bed?"

"I don't know."

"Why in the world do you want to marry her then?"

"Because she can still drive!"

✽ AN OLD MAN IS TAKING the road test to renew his driver's license. The instructor tells the old man that when she taps on the dashboard she wants him to slow down and show her the action he'd take if a young child ran out in front of his car. The instructor taps the dashboard a few minutes into the ride. The old man screeches the car to a halt, puts down the window, and yells to the empty street, "Be careful where you're going, you little jerk!"

✽ AN OLDER WOMAN GOES TO a gym because she wants to start taking a yoga class.

"I'm not sure that's a good idea at your age," the instructor says. "How flexible are you?"

"I'm very flexible," the old woman claims. "The only day I can't make is Tuesday."

✽ AN OLDER COUPLE LIVED TOGETHER in a small village for more than sixty years. To celebrate their anniversary, the husband took his wife to the big city for a night out on the town. They checked into a plush hotel, but had a complaint as soon as they checked in. The man said to the hotel manager, "We refuse to settle for such a small room! There are no windows, no bed, and no air-conditioning in our room either."

"But . . ." replied the hotel manager.

"Don't 'but' me," he continued. "You can't treat us like we're a couple of country fools just because we don't travel much. Even though we've never been to the big city, and never spent the night at a hotel, I'm not going to be played for a fool!"

"But sir!" the manager finally got out. "This isn't your room. This is the elevator."

✳ A NURSE CALLS A PATIENT to confirm her appointment for the next day.

"Hello, this is Dr. Cuban's office. I'm calling to speak with Anna."

"Lana?" the voice on the phone says back.

"Anna," the nurse responds.

"Santa?" the woman says back.

"Anna!" the nurse says a little louder.

"What's this about again?" the woman asks.

"This is Dr. Cuban's office, I'm calling to speak with Anna!"

"Oh Anna!" the woman replies. "This is her sister. You better speak with me. She's a little hard of hearing."

✳ A REAL ESTATE AGENT IS trying to sell an old man a new home.

"It's an incredible investment," the agent tells the old man over the phone. "The house will be worth double what you paid in just a few years."

"You're joking, right?" The old man laughs. "At my age it's a risk to even buy green bananas."

✳ A YOUNG MAN PASSES AN elderly man crying on a park bench. The young man stops and asks if everything is okay. The old man looks up with his eyes filled with tears.

"Kid," the old man says, "I'm ninety years old. Last week I married a woman half my age. She does everything for me—she cooks my meals, washes my clothes, shops for me, and will do anything I ask in the bedroom."

"Oh," replies the young man. "Well, that doesn't sound bad at all. Why are you sitting here crying?"

"Because," the old man sobs loudly. "I can't remember where the hell I live!"

* AN OLD MAN WAS FITTED with brand-new hearing aids. His hearing was better than it was in his prime. He returned to the clinic a week after the fitting and the audiologist asked him, "How are your hearing aids working?"

The old man replied, "They are fantastic. They work so well I've changed my will three times since last week."

* A MAN HAS BEEN MADLY in love with a woman since the day they met in kindergarten. He is much too shy to propose to her. They are both up in years and neither has ever been married. So he finally asks her out. They date about once a week for over six years, but he is so timid he never gets around to suggesting marriage, much less living together. One day, finally fed up with his shyness, he becomes determined to pop the question. He calls her on the phone at work and says, "June, will you marry me?"

"Of course I will!" June says. "But first, who is this?"

* A LITTLE OLD LADY ANSWERS a knock at the door one morning, only to be confronted by a well-dressed young man carrying a vacuum cleaner.

"Good morning," says the young man. "If I could take a couple of minutes of your time, I would like to demonstrate the very latest in high-powered vacuum cleaners."

"Go away!" says the old lady. "I haven't got any money!" She then proceeds to close the door. Quick as a flash, the young man wedges his foot in the door and pushes it wide open.

"Don't be too hasty!" he says. "Not until you have at least seen my demonstration." And with that, he empties a bucket of horse manure onto her hallway carpet. "If this vacuum cleaner does not remove all traces of this horse manure from your carpet, Madam, I will personally eat the remainder."

The old lady steps back and says, "Well, let me get you a fork because they cut off my electricity this morning."

❋ THREE SENIOR CITIZENS ARE SITTING on a park bench complaining about their failing bodies. "Every morning, I get up at 6 A.M.," the first man explains, "and I try to pee, but nothing but a trickle comes out." The second man adds, "I get up at 6 A.M. too, and it feels like I've got to move my bowels, but I sit down on the toilet and nothing happens."

The third man chimes in the conversation and tells his friends, "I pee and move my bowels at exactly 7 A.M. every morning."

"That's not bad," the first man responds. "Why are you complaining?"

The third man admits, "The problem is I don't usually wake up until 8 A.M."

❋ A HUSBAND AND WIFE WAKE up one morning, and when the man leans over to kiss his wife, she yells in his face.

"Don't touch me! I'm dead."

"What are you talking about?" the husband asks. "We're both lying in bed. You can't be dead."

"I must be dead," the wife responds, "because I woke up this morning and nothing hurts."

Ailments

❋ AN ADORABLE OLD WOMAN VISITS the doctor. "Doctor, I have this problem with gas, but it really doesn't bother me too much. It never smells and is always silent. As a matter of fact, I've farted at least ten times since I've been here in your office. You didn't know I was farting because it doesn't smell and is silent."

The doctor says, "I see. Take these pills and come back to see me next week."

The next week the lady returns. "Doctor," she says, "I don't know what the heck you gave me, but now my farts, although still silent, stink terribly."

"Good," the doctor says. "Now that we've cleared up your sinuses, let's work on your hearing."

✱ THREE OLD FRIENDS, ALL WITH very bad hearing, meet on the corner.

"Isn't it windy?" the first man asks.

"No," says the second, "it's Thursday."

"Agreed," says the third man, "let's go grab a beer."

 Famous Funnies

> "A sixty-seven-year-old woman in Spain gave birth to twins over the weekend. The mother and babies are doing fine, but the doctor who delivered the babies is still really nauseous."—Conan O'Brien

✱ TWO MEN ARE DISCUSSING THE ailing health of their parents.

"I feel bad," the first man says. "My dad is senile. All he does is stare through the window all day long."

"That's an awful way to live," the second man responds.

"Yeah, I know," the man admits. "One day I should really let him in the house."

✱ AN OLD VILLAGER GOES TO visit a wizard to remove a curse placed on him more than forty years earlier. "In order for me to reverse the curse," the wizard explains, "I've got the know the exact phrasing of the original curse."

"That's simple," the man replies. "It was 'I now pronounce you husband and wife.'"

✱ AN OLD MAN IS BRAGGING to his roommate at the nursing home about his new hearing aid. The man goes on and on about how great the hearing aid is and how well he can hear with it.

"It was also very expensive," the man says to his friend.

"Well, good for you," his friend replies. "What kind is it?"

"What time is it? It's only 12:30," the man answers.

Nursing Homes

✱ A MAN GOES TO THE nursing home to visit his eighty-four-year-old father. While there he notices the nurse hand his father a cup of hot chocolate and a Viagra pill. The man asks the nurse, "Why are you doing that? At his age, what will either do for him?"

"The hot chocolate," the nurse explains, "will help him fall asleep faster."

"All right," the man replies, "and what about the Viagra?"

"That keeps him from rolling out of bed."

✱ A WIFE IS VISITING HER husband in a nursing home. He sneezes, and for the first time in his life, covers his mouth with his hand. "I'm so proud of you," his wife says. "You finally learned to put your hand in front of your mouth after all these years."

"Of course I have," her husband replies. "How else am I going to catch my teeth?"

✱ THE HEAD DOCTOR IN A nursing home is making the rounds with the night nurse. They reach the room of Mr. Swanson. "I'm worried about Mr. Swanson," the nurse confides to the doctor. "I think he might be losing his mind. Yesterday, he told me that when he has to go to the bathroom in the middle of the night, the good Lord turns the light on for him. When he's done, the Lord turns the light off."

"That's normal and I've seen it happen before," the doctor tells the nurse. "It just means he's peeing in his fridge again."

Death

✱ AFTER A PREACHER DIED AND went to heaven, he noticed a New York cab driver had been awarded a higher place than he. "I don't understand," he complained to God. "I devoted my entire life to my congregation."

God explained to him, "Our policy here in heaven is to reward results. Now, was your congregation well attuned to you whenever you gave a sermon?"

"Well," the minister had to admit, "some in the congregation fell asleep from time to time."

"Exactly," said God, "and when people rode in this man's taxi, they not only stayed wake, they even prayed."

✱ A MAN SITS AT A bar just looking at his drink. He stays like that for half an hour. A massive, trouble-making truck driver steps next to him, takes the drink from the guy, and just drinks it all down. The poor man starts crying.

The truck driver says, "Come on, man, I was just joking. Here, I'll buy you another drink. I just can't stand to see a man cry."

"No, it's not that. This is the worst day of my life. First, I oversleep, and I get to my office late. My boss, outraged, fires me. When I leave the building I find out my car was stolen. The police say there's nothing they can do. I get a cab to return home, and when I leave it, I remember I left my wallet and credit cards there. The cab driver just drives away. I go home, and when I get there, I find my wife in bed with the gardener. I leave home, and come to this bar. And just when I was thinking about putting an end to my life, you show up and drink my poison."

✱ DID YOU HEAR THE GOOD news about reincarnation? It's making a comeback.

✴ A MAN DIES AND FINDS himself in front of God. He sees Jesus sitting at his right hand and a janitor with a mop sitting to his left. "Who are you?" the man asks the janitor.

"I'm Cleanliness."

 Famous Funnies

> "The inventor of the Etch A Sketch died last week. His family was shaken, but is now ready to start over."—Chris Illuminati

✴ A MAN PLACES SOME FLOWERS on the grave of his dearly departed mother and starts back toward his car when his attention is diverted to another man kneeling at a grave. The man seems to be praying with profound intensity and keeps repeating, "Why did you have to die? Why did you have to die?"

The first man approaches him and says, "Sir, I don't wish to interfere with your private grief, but this demonstration of pain is more than I've ever seen before. Who are you mourning? A child? A parent?"

The mourner takes a moment to collect himself, then replies, "My wife's first husband."

✴ A GUY DIES, GOES TO hell, and meets Satan. Satan says to the man, "Nowadays, people entering hell are able to choose their own personal hell. I will take you to a series of doors, and you will look inside, and tell me if that is where you would like to spend eternity."

The man agrees and Satan takes him down a long, dark hallway. Satan opens the first door, the man looks inside, and sees thousands of people standing on their heads on a hardwood floor.

The man says, "This looks too uncomfortable. Show me the next room please."

Satan then walks the man down to the second door. The man looks inside, and sees thousands of people standing on their heads on a concrete floor.

The man says, "This is even worse. Please show me another room."

Satan nods and takes him to the third door, and the man looks inside; he sees thousands of people standing knee-deep in liquid feces, all drinking coffee.

The man says, "This is the place for me."

Satan then asks, "Are you sure? Once the door closes you can never go back."

The man says, "I'm positive. I love coffee." The man steps in, and Satan closes the door. Just before the man can get comfortable, a voice on the loudspeaker says, "Coffee break is over. Back on your heads!"

✳ A MAN IS ON HIS deathbed and calls his business partner to his bedside. "I've got some things to tell you," the man says, gasping for breath. "I've been an awful partner. I've embezzled over $10 million from the company in the last five years, made a few million more selling our secrets to competitors, and I fired the receptionist because I knew she was in love with you."

His partner tells him, "That's fine. I forgive you, my friend. Just as long as you forgive me."

"Forgive you for what?" the dying man asks.

"I'm the one who poisoned you," his partner replies.

✳ ONE DARK NIGHT, TWO MEN are walking home after a party and decide to take a shortcut through the cemetery. Right in the middle of the cemetery they are startled by a tap-tap-tapping noise coming from the misty shadows. Trembling with fear, they find an old man with a hammer and chisel, chipping away at one of the headstones.

"Holy cow, dude," one says after catching his breath. "You scared us half to death. We thought you were a ghost! What are you doing, working here so late at night?"

"Those fools!" the old man grumbles. "They misspelled my name!"

Famous Funnies

"I am not afraid of death, I just don't want to be there when it happens."—Woody Allen

✳ TED AND STEVE ARE BEST friends. They made an agreement at a very early age that if one of them died, he'd come back and tell the other what it was like in the afterlife. Finally, after ninety years Ted passes away, leaving Steve alone. A few nights after Ted dies, he appears to Steve in the middle of the night.

"Steve. Steve!" The dead man speaks from somewhere in the distance. Steve sits up in bed.

"Ted, is that you?"

"Yes, it's me! I'm here to tell you about the afterlife. It's amazing!"

"Tell me about it!" Steve begs.

"Well," Ted begins, "every morning I get up, get something small to eat, then spend all morning making love. Then we have lunch and spend more time making love. Then we have dinner and do the same thing all over again."

"My God!" Steve cries out. "Heaven sounds fantastic."

"Heaven?" Ted responds. "I'm outside your window. I came back as a rabbit."

✳ A MAN CONGRATULATES HIS NEIGHBOR on his ninetieth birthday. "You look fantastic for your age!" he tells the old man.

"Thanks," he replies, "but I'm actually only eighty. Since my wife died last week, it feels like every day is my birthday!"

✳ A MAN IS FIXING HIS hair in his wife's compact mirror when he accidentally drops it on the ground. "Oh great," he says, "there's seven years of bad luck."

"Not necessarily," the wife tells her husband. "My uncle once broke a massive wall mirror and he didn't have seven years of bad luck."

"Really?" the man asks, feeling a little better about the accident.

"Nope," she continues, "he dropped the mirror on his head and died instantly."

✳ A NEW BUSINESS IS OPENING and one of the owner's friends wants to send him flowers for the occasion. They arrive at the new business site and the owner reads the card: "Rest in Peace." Understandably the owner is angry and calls the florist to complain.

After he tells the florist of the obvious mistake and how angry he is, the florist replies, "Sir, I'm really sorry for the mistake, but rather than getting angry, you should imagine this. Somewhere there is a funeral taking place today, and they have flowers with a note saying, 'Congratulations on your new location.'"

✳ A HUSBAND CALLS FOR HIS wife on his deathbed. He tells his wife that after he passes away he doesn't want her to be alone. "Six months after I pass, I think it would be okay for you to marry Joe."

"Joe?" his wife asks. "But I thought you hated Joe."

"I do," the man answers.

 Comedy Facts

Research has shown conclusively that humans laugh more in social situations than when alone. In a crowd, female audience members laugh more often than their male counterparts.

✳ A COUPLE'S HAPPY MARRIED LIFE almost goes completely wrong because of Aunt Emma. For seventeen long years, Aunt

Emma has lived with them, always crotchety, always demanding. Finally, the old woman passes away. On the way back from the cemetery, the husband confesses to his wife, "Darling, if I didn't love you so much, I don't think I would have put up with having your Aunt Emma in the house all those years."

His wife looks at him in shock.

"My Aunt Emma?" she cries. "I thought she was your Aunt Emma!"

✽ A CULT OF CANNIBALS EATS a car full of circus clowns. In the middle of the meal one cannibal turns to the other and asks, "Does this meal taste funny to you?"

✽ THERE ONCE WAS AN OLD man who worked in a whiskey distillery. One night, while working late, he tripped over his shoelaces and fell into a massive vat of booze. Six hours later he drowned. It really shouldn't have taken as long as it did for him to die, but he got out of the vat three times to take a leak.

✽ A FATHER PASSES AWAY AND his son is arranging the funeral. He talks to the mortician about his father's remains.

The son says, "I know we don't have much money, but I want the best for my father. Please do what you can."

A week after the funeral, the mortician presents the son with a bill for fifty dollars. Thinking it to be very reasonable, the son pays the bill. The next week, the son gets another bill for fifty dollars from the mortician. He pays that as well. A week later a third bill arrives in the amount of fifty dollars.

The son calls the mortician and says, "The funeral was three weeks ago. Why am I still getting bills for fifty dollars?"

"You wanted the best for your father," the mortician says, "so that tux was rented."

✽ TWO MEN ARE TALKING ABOUT how they want to leave the world.

"I'd like to go out like my uncle," says the first man. "He died at the race track."

The second man says he'd like to go out like his grandfather. "He just died peacefully. Fell asleep and never woke up or made a sound. Nothing like the people riding in his bus."

✱ AN ELDERLY MAN ON HIS deathbed tells his wife, "Honey, I want you to promise me that when I go you will put all my money in the casket with me."

Reluctantly, his wife agrees and assures him she will uphold her promise. After the funeral, the woman tells her friend about her husband's odd request. "You know, he made me swear to bury all our money with him."

The friend replies, "That's crazy! I can't believe you would actually do that."

The elderly woman says, "Don't worry. I wrote him a check."

✱ A MAN IS VERY SURPRISED at the empty seat next to him at the Super Bowl. He notices a woman sitting next to the empty seat and makes a remark about it to her.

"Well, it was my husband's," she says. "But he died."

"Oh my gosh!" he says. "I'm sorry for your loss, but I'm surprised that another friend or family member didn't jump at the chance to take the ticket."

"Beats me," she says. "They all insisted on going to the funeral."

✱ A MAN WAS LEAVING A convenience store with his morning coffee when he noticed a most unusual funeral procession approaching the nearby cemetery. A black hearse drove by, followed by a second black hearse, about 50 feet behind the first one. Behind the second hearse was a solitary man walking a dog on a leash. Behind him, a short distance back, were about 200 men walking single file. The man couldn't stand the curiosity. He respectfully approached the man walking the dog and said: "I am so sorry for your loss, and this may be a bad time to disturb you, but I've never seen a funeral like this. Whose funeral is it?"

"My wife's."

The man was shocked. "What happened to her?"

"She yelled at me and my dog attacked and killed her."

The man inquired further, "Well, who is in the second hearse?"

The man walking the dog answered, "That's my mother-in-law. She was trying to help my wife when the dog turned on her. She didn't survive either."

A silence passed between the two men. "Can I borrow the dog?"

The man holding the leash replied, "Get in line."

✳ TWO MEN DIED AND WENT to heaven. God greeted them and said, "I'm sorry, gentlemen, but your mansions aren't ready yet. Until they are, I can send you back to earth to be whatever you want to be."

"Great!" said the first guy. "I want to be a famous movie star!"

"No problem," replied God. "Poof." The guy was gone.

"And what do you want to be?" God asked the other guy.

"I'd like to be one cool stud!"

"Easy," replied God. "Poof." The guy was gone.

After a few months, their mansions were finished and God sent an angel to fetch them back.

"You'll find them easily," God told the angel. "One of them is in Hollywood and the other one is on a snow tire somewhere in Detroit."

✳ THREE FRIENDS DIE IN A car accident and go to heaven for an orientation. They are asked, "When you were in your casket, and friends and family were mourning over you, what would you have liked them to say about you?"

The first guy says, "I would have liked to hear them say, 'He was a great doctor and a great family man.'"

The second guy says, "I would have liked to hear them say, 'He was a wonderful husband and teacher who made a huge difference in many children's lives.'"

The last guy says, "I would have liked to hear them say, 'Look, he's moving!'"

✳ A MAN FINDS HIS FRIEND at the bar, depressed and nursing a vodka. "What's the matter?" he asks.

"Well," the man begins, taking a sip, "in April, my mother passed away and left me $10,000. In May, my dad passed away and left $20,000."

"Man, that's awful," the second man consoles his friend.

"It gets worse," the sad man continues, "in June, my great-aunt passed away and left me $50,000." The man took another sip of his drink and said, "So, here it is, the middle of July and no one else in my family has died yet."

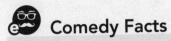 **Comedy Facts**

Hunter Doherty Adams, better known by his nickname "Patch," is an American physician, social activist, clown, and author who founded the Gesundheit! Institute. Each year, Adams organizes a group of volunteers to travel to various impoverished countries. The volunteers dress as clowns in an effort to bring humor to orphans, patients, and other people suffering in the world's poorest areas. The 1998 movie *Patch Adams* was based on his work.

✳ TWO GUYS SHOW UP IN heaven at the same time. The first guy says he froze to death, and the second guy tells the first that he died of a heart attack.

"How did that happen?" asks the first guy.

"Well, I came home and thought I heard my wife with another man. But when I searched the house, I couldn't find anybody. I was so stricken with remorse for wrongly accusing my wife of infidelity, I had a heart attack and died on the spot."

"Geez," says the first guy. "If you'd opened the fridge, we'd both be alive right now."

✳ TWO OLD MEN ARE OUT on the golf course one morning playing their usual round of golf when a funeral procession comes down the street next to the green. One of the old men notices the procession and immediately stops in the middle of his putt. He calmly steps away from his ball, removes his cap, and bows his head in silence as the procession passes by. The other old man is amazed at his friend's reverence for the deceased.

"That was truly one of the most touching and thoughtful acts I've ever seen from you," he says.

"Well I figure it's the least I could do. After all, we were married for forty-two years."

CHAPTER 9

Animals and Pets

The following jokes about our four-legged friends will make even those who don't like animals very much chuckle. After all, animals can be just as crazy and hilarious as their human counterparts. These amusing anecdotes and ridiculous gags are sure to make anyone smirk like the Cheshire cat or laugh like a hyena.

✻ A MAN ANGRILY KNOCKS ON the door of a house. The homeowner answers and the man begins shouting, "Your dog jumped the fence, chased me on a bicycle, and bit my leg!"

The homeowner looks at the man and says, "That's impossible. My dog has no idea how to ride a bike."

✻ THERE WAS A FATHER MOLE, a mother mole, and a baby mole that lived in a hole out in the country not far from a farmhouse. One morning, the father mole poked his head out of the hole and said, "Mmmm, I think I smell sausage cooking!"

The mother mole pushed the father mole aside, poked her head outside the hole, and said, "Mmmm, I think I smell pancakes!"

The baby mole tried to push aside the two bigger moles to stick his head outside the hole, but couldn't, because he was so much smaller.

Frustrated, the baby mole said out loud, "The only thing I smell is molasses."

❋ A PIG WALKS INTO A bar, orders twenty beers, and starts chugging them all one by one. "That's impressive," says the bartender. "Want to know where the bathroom is?"

The pig replies, "No thanks, pal. I'm just going to go wee wee wee all the home."

❋ HOW DOES AN OCTOPUS GO to war? Very well armed.

❋ WHY WAS THE DUCK ARRESTED? He was suspected of selling quack.

❋ TWO ROACHES ARE MUNCHING ON garbage in an alley when one starts a discussion about a new restaurant.

"I was in that new restaurant across the street," says one. "It's so clean! The kitchen is spotless, and the floors are gleaming white. There is no dirt anywhere—it's so sanitary that the whole place shines."

"Please," says the other roach, frowning. "Not while I'm eating!"

❋ DID YOU HEAR ABOUT THE breakdancing goldfish? He could only do it for about twenty seconds.

❋ WHAT DID THE FATHER BUFFALO say to his kid before leaving for work every morning? Bison.

 Comedy Facts

More than a few studies have shown that animals do have the ability to laugh. Monkeys, dogs, and even rats have all exhibited the same characteristics as humans do during joyous moments. When chimps play together they pant in a way that's similar to the human laugh. Rats chirp in much the same way.

❋ TWO FLIES LAND ON A pile of manure. One fly passes gas. The other fly looks at him and says, "Hey do you mind? I'm eating here."

✴ A MAN WALKS INTO A zoo. The only animal in the entire zoo is a dog. It's a shih tzu.

✴ A MOTHER BUNNY WAS SHOPPING with her little bunny when finally she had enough of the little bunny's question. "A magician pulled you out of a hat! Now stop asking!"

✴ TWO MEN, JIM AND JOHN, are walking their dogs when they pass by a restaurant.

"Let's go in and get something to eat," Jim suggests.

"We can't," responds John. "Don't you see the sign says *No Pets Allowed*?"

"Oh that sign?" says Jim. "Don't worry about it."

Taking out a pair of sunglasses, he walks up to the door. As he tries walking into the restaurant, the host says, "Sorry, no pets allowed."

"Can't you see," says Jim, "I am blind. This is my Seeing Eye dog."

"But it's a Doberman pinscher. Who uses a Doberman pinscher as a Seeing Eye dog?" the host asks.

"Oh," Jim responds, "you must not have heard. This is the latest type of Seeing Eye dog. They do a very good job."

Seeing that it worked, John tries walking in with his Chihuahua. Even before he can open his mouth, the host says, "Don't tell me that a Chihuahua is the latest type of Seeing Eye dog."

John responds angrily, "You mean they gave me a Chihuahua?"

✴ A SNAKE GOES IN TO see the optometrist because his eyesight is failing.

"It's actually affecting my life. I can't hunt anymore because I can't see."

The doctor fits the snake for glasses and the snake immediately notices an improvement in his eyesight. A week later, the doctor calls the snake to check how the glasses are holding up.

"They're fine," the snake answers. "But now I'm being treated for depression." "Depression?" the doctor asks.

"Yeah, my eyesight cleared up, but it made me realize I've been dating a garden hose."

✱ TWO DUCKS ARE HAVING AN affair. They rent a hotel room for an hour, but the male duck forgot contraception. He calls down to room service.

"Got it," says the front desk, "and would you like these on your bill?"

"Of course not," the duck says. "I'd suffocate."

✱ WHY DON'T BLIND PEOPLE SKYDIVE? It scares the crap out of the dog.

✱ WHAT DID THE TERMITE SAY when he walked into the tavern? "Is the bar tender here?"

✱ A LADY WAS EXPECTING THE plumber. He was scheduled to come at 10 A.M. Ten o'clock came and went with no plumber. She concluded he wasn't coming, and went out to do some errands. While she was out, the plumber arrived. He knocked on the door; the lady's parrot, who was at home in a cage by the door, said, "Who is it?"

He replied, "It's the plumber."

He thought it was the lady who'd said, "Who is it?" and waited for her to come and let him in.

When this didn't happen he knocked again, and again the parrot said, "Who is it?"

He said, "It's the plumber!" He waited, and again the lady didn't come to let him in.

He knocked again, and again the parrot said, "Who is it?"

He said, "It's the plumber!"

Again he waited and again she didn't come. He knocked again and the parrot said, "Who is it?"

The plumber screamed, flew into a rage, pushed the door in, and ripped it off its hinges. He suffered a heart attack and fell dead in the doorway. The lady came home from her errands, only to see the door ripped off its hinges and a corpse lying in the doorway. "A dead body!" she exclaimed. "Who is it?"

The parrot said, "It's the plumber."

✱ THERE ONCE WAS A GUY who was going on a date to the movies with a beautiful girl. Before he left, he made the mistake of eating a jumbo can of beans. Right after he picked her up, he felt the need to fart, but he figured he could wait until they got to the movies. When they got there, he asked her if she wanted some popcorn and Coke. She said sure, so he went to the restroom. The line was long, so he went back to the lobby, got the food, and went back into the theater. When the movie was over, he goes to the bathroom again, still with a tremendously long line. So he figured he could wait until he dropped her off. When they pulled up into her driveway, she exclaimed, "Oh good. My grandparents are here. Come on in and meet them."

He agreed, although he was about to cry at this point. They went in and sat down at the table. Finally, he couldn't hold it in any longer, and tried to let it seep out a little at a time. As he squeezed out a toxic blast, he aimed it toward the family's hound dog Duke, in hopes that they might blame the pooch for the horrendous fart. The girl's father stood up and hollered, "Duke!" and sat back down.

"Great!" he thought. "They really think it's the dog!" So, he started bombarding the room with a couple of more powerful, louder stinkers.

Once again, the girl's father stood up, shouted "Duke!" and sat back down.

Finally, he let it all go. The loudest, most hair-curling fart you've ever heard or smelled rippled through the dining room. The girl's father stood up again. "Duke, get the hell out from under him before he poops on you!"

✱ TWO COWS ARE SITTING IN the field when one says, "Hey man, I've been hearing a lot of bad stuff lately. Are you worried about this 'Mad Cow Disease'?"

The other cow starts to spin around with his hooves extended out and says, "Not me, pal. I'm a helicopter."

 Famous Funnies

> "I ask people why they have deer heads on their walls. They always say because it's such a beautiful animal. There you go. I think my mother is attractive, but I have photographs of her."—Ellen DeGeneres

✱ A CHICKEN WALKS OVER TO a duck standing on the side of the road. The duck is considering crossing to the other side.

"Don't do it, pal," the chicken says. "You'll never hear the end of it."

✱ THREE VAMPIRE BATS LIVE IN a cave surrounded by three castles. One night, the bats bet on who can drink the most blood. The first bat comes home with blood dripping off his fangs.

He says, "See that castle over there? I drank the blood of three people."

The second bat returns with blood around his mouth. He says, "See that castle over there? I drank the blood of five people."

The third bat comes back covered in blood. He says, "See that castle over there?" The other bats nod. "Well," says the third bat, "I didn't."

 Famous Funnies

> "My wife kisses the dog on the lips yet won't even drink from my glass."—Rodney Dangerfield

✳ WHAT DO YOU GET WHEN you cross a lion with a parrot? No idea, but when that animal talks, people will listen.

✳ DAVE WENT TO THE STORE for a box of mothballs. His closet was infested with moths and he needed a solution. The next day, Dave returned to buy five more boxes.

"Weren't you just here yesterday to buy a box of mothballs?" the store clerk asked.

"Yes, but I used up that box already. Those suckers are hard to hit when they start moving!"

✳ WHY DID THE CHICKEN SAY, "Meow, oink, bow-wow, and moo"? He was studying foreign languages.

✳ WHY DID THE ANTS DANCE on the top of the jam jar? The top said, "Twist to Open."

✳ WHY CAN'T YOU HEAR A pterodactyl in the bathroom? Because it has a silent pee.

✳ WHAT DID THE LITTLE FISH say when he swam into a wall? *DAM!*

✳ WHAT DO YOU CALL A deer with no eyes? No eye deer.

✳ WHY DON'T COWS EVER HAVE money? Because farmers milk them dry.

✳ TWO FARMERS ARE STANDING IN a field discussing their work.

"I'm having an issue with my flock of cows," the first farmer admits.

"Herd of cows," the second farmer corrects his friend.

"Of course I've heard of cows," the first farmer barks, "I've got a whole flock of them!"

✳ WHAT DID THE GRAPE SAY when an elephant stepped on it? Nothing, it just let out a little wine.

✳ "JULIE," HER MOTHER ASKED, "WHY are you feeding bird seed to the cat?"

"Because," Julie answered, "that's where my canary is."

✳ A MAN RINGS THE DOORBELL of a small house and an old woman answers.

"I'm sorry," the man says, "but I'm afraid I've run over your cat. I'd like to replace it if I can."

"All right," the old woman says. "But how good are you at catching mice?"

✳ A COUPLE'S HOUSE IS INFESTED with flies. While waiting for the exterminator, the husband goes around the house on a mission to kill as many flies as possible.

"Well," he says to his wife, "I killed six flies. Four were male and two were female."

"How can you tell the sex?" she asks.

"Four of the flies were on a beer can and the other two were on the phone."

✳ A BOY ASKS HIS FATHER for a spider for his birthday. The father stops by the pet shop on the way home from work to find out more about spiders.

"What does one of those big ones cost?" the father asks, pointing into the glass case full of the arachnids.

"About fifty dollars," the store clerk replies.

"Fifty dollars!" the father replies. "I'll just find a cheap one off the web."

✳ WHAT DO BEES SAY ABOUT the summer weather? Swarm.

✳ WHY DID THE EAGLE GROW his claws so long? He wanted to enter a local talon contest.

✳ WHAT IS THE NUMBER ONE cause of death for hamsters? Falling asleep at the wheel.

✳ AL BRAGGED ABOUT HIS HOME aquarium to a friend.

"I keep it super clean," he said. "And my fish are always so darn happy."

"How the heck can you tell your fish are happy?" his friend asked.

"Because," Al replied, "they are always wagging their tails."

 Ask the Comedian

Is telling a joke I heard on a talk show or read online stealing?
It all depends on the venue in which you're telling the joke. If you're retelling a joke to a group of coworkers or delivering a one-liner to the mailman, there is no harm in recounting another comedian's material. It would be absurd to credit the original author after every witty comment or pun you picked up from somewhere else. Now, if you're going on stage and delivering the material of another comic, that is absolutely stealing.

✳ A GRASSHOPPER WALKS INTO A crowded bar. He sits down on a stool and orders a glass of beer. The bartender says, "That's funny. I figured you'd order something different, especially since we've got a drink named after you."

The grasshopper looks at the bartender baffled and says, "You've got a drink named Stan?"

✳ A MAN IS SITTING ON his couch watching TV when he hears the doorbell ring. He opens the door, and all he can see is a snail sitting on his front porch. He throws the snail across the street and goes back to watching TV. A year later, he is again sitting on his couch watching TV when the doorbell rings again. He opens the door to see an angry snail, who yells, "What the heck was that for?"

✳ A CHICKEN WALKS INTO A library, approaches the main library desk, and says: "Book! Book! Booooooook!" The librarian hands over two popular paperbacks, and watches the chicken as it leaves the library, walks across the street, goes through a field, and disappears over a hill.

The next day, the chicken returns to the library. The chicken walks right up to the librarian, drops the old books on her desk, and says, "Book! Book! Boooooook!" The librarian hands over a few hardback books and again watches the chicken drag them away, across the street, through the field, and over the hill.

On the third day, the chicken returns, drops the books on the desk, and says, "Book! Book! Boooooook!" This time, once the chicken is out the door, the librarian follows—across the street, through the field, over the hill, and down to a small pond. On a rock at the edge of the pond is the biggest frog the librarian has ever seen. The chicken walks up to the frog, drops the books at the frog's feet, and says, "Book! Book! Boooooook!"

The frog hops up and down, uses his front leg to push through the pile, and says: "Read It! Read It! Read It!"

✳ WHY DO POLAR BEARS HAVE fur coats? Because leather jackets would look really ridiculous.

✳ TWO BATS ARE HANGING UPSIDE down in a cave. The first bat asks the second, "Do you remember the worst day of your life?"

The second bat replies, "I sure do. It was the day I had diarrhea."

✳ A KANGAROO KEEPS ESCAPING HIS enclosure at the zoo. In an effort to keep him inside at night, the zookeepers construct a 10-foot fence around his habitat. The next morning, they find the kangaroo wandering around the zoo. The zookeepers construct a 20-foot fence to keep the kangaroo from escaping, but the next day he is loose once again. The zookeepers begin construction on a 50-foot fence they're sure will keep the kangaroo in his enclosure. Watching the men work, a camel in the neighboring enclosure sticks his head over to the kangaroo's side and asks, "How high do you think they'll make it this time?"

The kangaroo answers, "Not sure, but it still won't matter, unless they remember to lock the door this time."

✸ A ZOOKEEPER STUMBLES ACROSS A man throwing five-dollar bills into the monkey cage.

"What the heck are you doing?" the zookeeper asks.

"The signs says it's cool," the man answers, pointing to a sign in front of the cages.

"No, it doesn't," the zookeeper replies.

"Sure it does," says the man, tossing another bill in the cage. "It says, 'Do Not Feed Monkeys. $5 Fine.'"

✸ DID YOU HEAR ABOUT THE leopard constantly trying to escape the national zoo? It never works; he's constantly spotted.

✸ A BLIND MAN IS WALKING down the street with his Seeing Eye dog. They stop at the corner to wait for the traffic light to change. The dog, unable to wait any longer, begins peeing on the blind man's leg. After the dog finishes, the blind man reaches into his coat pocket and pulls out a doggie treat. He holds it out for the dog. A pedestrian standing next to the blind man sees the entire event and he's shocked. He turns to the blind man and says, "Why would you reward your dog for peeing on your leg?"

The blind man replies, "Oh I'm not rewarding him, I'm just trying to find his head so I can kick him in the butt."

✸ HOW DID THE FISH GET high? He's got a connection for really good seaweed.

✸ A WOMAN CALLS THE VET because her beloved dog isn't moving. The vet makes a house call and after a quick examination, the vet tells the woman her dog is going to die.

"Isn't there anything you can do?" the woman pleads with the vet. He thinks it over, leaves the room, and returns with her cat. The cat sniffs the dog head to toe, looks him over, and shakes his head at the vet.

"I'm sorry, miss. It's out of our hands." The vet hands the woman a bill before he leaves for $1,570.

"What?" the woman screams. "How is the bill $1,570? You didn't do anything."

"Well," replies the vet, "it's $70 for the consultation, $100 for the house call, and $1,400 for the emergency cat scan."

✳ A MAN GOES TO A store for some laundry detergent. He tells the man working the register it's for his filthy dog. "I'm not sure you're supposed to wash animals in laundry detergent," the guy behind the register says. The man leaves with the detergent and comes back a week later to get groceries.

"How's your dirty dog?" the worker asks.

"Oh, he died," replies the man.

"I told you washing your dog in detergent was an awful idea!" the man exclaims. "Relax," says the dog owner. "I'm pretty sure it was the spin cycle that killed him."

✳ A PENGUIN WALKS INTO A bar and asks the barkeep, "Have you seen my brother?" The bartender says, "I'm not sure. What does he look like?"

✳ A FARMER SPENDS $7,000 ON a young registered Black Angus bull to mate with his cows. He puts the bull out with the herd, but the animal just eats grass. He won't even look at the cows. The farmer feels cheated, so he brings in the local vet to check out the bull. The bull is very healthy, the vet explains, but possibly just a little young. So he gives the farmer pills to feed the bull once per day. It will help with his urge to mate. After a few days, the bull starts to service a few cows, and within a week, every cow on the farm. The bull even breaks through the fence and breeds with all of the neighbor's cows. He turns into a mating machine. A friend of the farmer asks exactly what the vet gave the bull to cause such a drastic change.

"I don't know exactly what was in those pills," the farmer says. "All I can tell you is they work and they taste like peppermint."

✳ A MAN IS TELLING A bartender about the craziest day of his life.

"It was unreal," the man recalls. "I'm on this horse that's galloping at top speed. On the right side of me is this elephant going as fast as the horse. Right in front of us is another horse going just fast enough so we don't hit him, and about ten feet behind us is a lion giving chase. He could catch us at any minute!"

The bartender is in shock. "My God," he says to the man. "What did you do?"

"Well I had no choice," the man replies, taking a sip of his beer. "I got my drunk butt off that merry-go-round as fast as possible."

✳ A BURGLAR BREAKS INTO A house late at night. He's going through all of the family's belongings when he hears a voice say, "Jesus is watching you."

He looks around and sees no one, and thinks he's imagining things. He goes back to what he's doing and again hears a voice say, "Jesus is watching you."

He shines his flashlight on a parrot in a cage across the room. "Are you the one saying 'Jesus is watching me'?" he asks the parrot.

"Yes," the parrot replies.

"What's your name?" the burglar asks.

"My name is Clarence."

"Clarence?" The burglar laughs. "That's a dumb name for a parrot. What idiot named you Clarence?"

The parrot answers, "The same idiot who named his pit bull Jesus."

✳ A MAN ON VACATION IN the Caribbean decides to go horseback riding. He visits a local farm that rents horses to ride around the countryside. The owner of the horse, a very religious man, explains to the visitor that in order to make the horse go, he'll have to say "Thank God," and to make the horse stop, he should say "Amen."

During his ride around the village, the horse is stung by a bee. In pain and shock, the horse takes off running right toward a dangerous cliff.

"Amen!" the man shouts, hanging on to the horse for dear life. The horse stops just a few inches short of the cliff's edge. The man catches his breath, looks over the cliff, and mutters out loud, "Thank God."

✳ A MAN BUYS A TALKING parrot from the local pet shop. He takes the parrot home and tries to teach the parrot to say a few things. Instead of repeating him, the parrot just swears at the man. After a few aggravating hours of the same responses from the parrot, the man threatens the bird with a severe punishment.

"If you don't stop swearing, I'm going to put you in the freezer."

The parrot continues to curse, so the man has no choice but to put him in the freezer. About a half hour later, the man opens the door to find the parrot happy to see him but freezing cold.

"Have you learned your lesson?" the man asks.

"I sure have," the parrot replies. "I promise never to swear again."

After thawing out for a moment, the parrot turns to the man and asks, "So what did the turkey in there do to you?"

✳ WHAT'S THE DIFFERENCE BETWEEN DEER nuts and beer nuts? Beer nuts are a dollar seventy-five and deer nuts are always under a buck.

✳ A DOG WALKS INTO AN employment agency and says he's looking for full-time work. "Holy cow! A talking dog!" the agency owner cries. "With your talent, I'm sure we could find you a job in entertainment. Maybe a circus?"

"A circus?" the dog asks. "Why would the circus need an accountant?"

✳ A FROG GOES INTO A bank and approaches the teller. The name on her tag says her name is Patricia Whack.

"Miss Whack," the frog begins, "I'd like to apply for a $30,000 loan to take a well-earned vacation." Patty looks at the frog in disbelief and asks his name.

The frog replies, "My name is Kermit. Kermit Jagger. My dad is Mick, and he knows the bank manager personally." Patty explains that he will need some type of collateral to secure the loan.

The frog says, "Sure. I have this," and pulls a tiny porcelain elephant from his briefcase. "My father got this as a gift in 1968 and it's been appraised for close to $200,000."

Very confused by the entire situation, Patty tells the frog that she'll have to consult with the bank manager and disappears into a back office.

She walks into the manager's office and says, "You're never going to believe this, but there's a frog sitting at my desk right now. He says his name is Kermit Jagger. He says he's the son of Mick Jagger, says his dad knows you, and he wants to borrow $30,000. He wants to use this as collateral." She holds up the tiny porcelain elephant. "I don't even know what it is!"

The bank manager looks at the figurine, then back at Patty, and tells her, "That's a knick-knack, Patty Whack. Give that frog a loan. His old man's a Rolling Stone."

 Famous Funnies

"You know when they have a fishing show on TV, they catch the fish and then let it go. They don't want to eat the fish, they just want to make it late for something."—Mitch Hedberg

✳ AFTER RETURNING FROM A TRIP from the Sunshine State, a man tells his friend all the things he'd seen. "Did you know in Florida they use alligators to make handbags?"

His friend says in amazement, "Wow, it's crazy what they can make animals do these days."

✱ A LOST DOG STRAYS INTO a jungle. A lion sees this from a distance and says with caution, "This guy looks edible; never seen his kind before." So the lion starts rushing toward the dog with menace. The dog notices and starts to panic, but as he's about to run he sees some bones next to him and gets an idea. He says loudly, "Mmm . . . that was some good lion meat!"

The lion abruptly stops and says, "Whoa! This guy seems tougher than he looks. I'd better leave while I can."

From a nearby treetop, a monkey witnesses everything. The monkey realizes that he can benefit from this situation by telling the lion and getting something in return, so he proceeds to tell the lion what really happened. The lion says angrily, "Get on my back, we'll get him together." They start rushing back to the dog. The dog sees them and, realizing what has happened, starts to panic even more.

He then gets another idea and shouts, "Where the hell is that monkey? I told him to bring me another lion an hour ago!"

CHAPTER 10

Everyday Life

Legendary comedian Will Rogers once said, "Everything is funny as long as it is happening to somebody else." Life is full of funny moments: Someone falling down, putting your foot in your mouth, getting caught in an uncomfortable situation with no easy way out. Here are some jokes about everyday life that will have you and your friends in stitches.

✳ THREE MEN ARE ON A hill. The first man throws his watch down the hill and it breaks into pieces. The second man throws his watch down the hill and it also breaks into pieces. The third man throws his watch down the hill, runs down to the bottom, and catches it before it hits the ground. His friends are amazed.

"How the heck did you do that?" asks the first man.

The third man replies, "It's pretty simple. My watch is five minutes slow."

✳ A MAN IS STUCK INSIDE a public restroom without any toilet paper. He calls over to the man in the next stall, "Hey, you got any extra toilet paper in there?"

"No," replies the man.

"You got any newspaper over there?" the stranded man asks.

"Nope," the second man replies.

After a moment of silence, the first man asks the second, "You got two fives for a ten?"

✳ TWO PRIESTS ARE STANDING BY the side of the road holding up a sign that reads, "The End Is Near! Turn yourself around now before it's too late!" They plan to hold up the sign to each passing car.

"Leave us alone, you religious nuts!" yells the first driver as he speeds by. From around the curve the priests hear screeching tires and a big splash.

"Do you think," one priest says to the other, "it would be better to shorten the sign to 'Bridge Out' instead?"

✳ TWO MEN ARE WALKING SIDE by side down the street. One of them sees a broken piece of mirror on the ground, grabs it, looks at it, and says, "This guy looks so familiar, but I can't remember where I know him from."

The other guy grabs it from his hand, takes a look at it, and says, "It's me, you idiot!"

✳ DID YOU HEAR ABOUT THE guy they found dead with his head in his cornflakes? The police think it's the work of a cereal killer.

✳ THE PAST, PRESENT, AND FUTURE walk into a bar. It was tense.

✳ AS AN AIRPLANE IS ABOUT to crash, a female passenger jumps up frantically and announces, "If I'm going to die, I want to die feeling like a woman."

She removes all her clothing and asks, "Is there someone on this plane who is man enough to make me feel like a woman?"

A man stands up, removes his shirt, and says, "Here, iron this!"

✳ WHILE GROCERY SHOPPING, A SINGLE man comes across toilet brushes.

"Wow! What a great idea," he thinks to himself, and buys three of them.

Two weeks later he goes back to using toilet paper.

✳ WHAT DID THE REDNECK SAY before he died? "Watch this! Hold my beer."

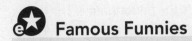

Famous Funnies

"A word to the wise isn't necessary. It's the stupid ones that need the advice."—Bill Cosby

✳ WHEN NASA FIRST STARTED SENDING up astronauts, they quickly discovered that many pens would not work in zero gravity. To combat this problem, NASA scientists spent a decade and over $12 billion in tax money developing a pen that writes in zero gravity, upside down, underwater, and on almost any surface including glass. The pen will work in temperatures ranging from below freezing to over 500°F. The Russians decided to just use a pencil.

✳ A SALESMAN RINGS THE DOORBELL to a small home. The door opens and a young boy stands in the doorway holding a cigarette in one hand and a can of beer in the other hand. Knowing the boy is way too young to be doing either, the salesman asks, "Is your mom home?"

The boy takes a swig of beer and replies, "What do you think?"

✳ A TEACHER HAS A CLASS full of rednecks. She asks someone to use the word "Timbuktu" in a story. A scrawny kid in the back raises his hand and says proudly, "Tim and me went hiking. Till we found three girls in a pitch-up tent. They were three and we were two. So I buck one and Tim buck two!"

✳ A MAN IS PULLED OVER for speeding. The cop asks to search his car and finds a case full of daggers in the back seat.

"What are all these for?" the cop asks.

"I'm a professional juggler," the man explains, "and those are a part of my act."

"I don't believe you," the skeptical cop says.

"Fine," says the man, "I'll prove it to you." He removes the daggers from the case and begins to juggle them on the side of the road. Two men in a passing car notice the performance. The driver turns to his friend in the passenger seat and comments, "Boy, I'm so glad I stopped drinking. The field sobriety tests are getting harder every year."

 ## Comedy Facts

Laughter tends to happen in short, vowel-like bursts of sound. These "ha-ha" and "ho-ho" sounds are often repeated every fifth of a second. Most people can't laugh on command, and laughter is not something humans can produce consciously. Laughter is, however, extremely contagious.

✳ HOW MANY AMERICAN TOURISTS DOES it take to change a light bulb? Fifteen. Five to figure out how much the bulb costs in the local currency, four to comment on "how funny-looking" local light bulbs are, three to hire a local person to change the bulb, two to take pictures, and one to buy postcards in case the pictures don't come out.

✳ YOU MIGHT BE A REDNECK if your daughter's sweet sixteen is sponsored by Budweiser.

✳ FOUR OLD CATHOLIC WOMEN SIT and brag about their sons. The first woman tells her friends, "My son is a priest. When he walks into a room, everyone calls him 'Father.'"

The second woman chirps, "My son is a bishop. Whenever he walks into a room, people call him 'Your Grace.'"

The third mother says, "My son is a cardinal. Whenever he walks into a room, he's called 'Your Eminence.'"

The fourth woman says, "My incredibly handsome son is six foot two with broad, square shoulders, good manners, and impeccable style. Whenever he walks into a room, women say, 'Oh my God!'"

✳ WHEN IS A DOOR SWEET and tasty? When it's jammed!

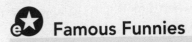 **Famous Funnies**

> "I hope we find a cure for every major disease because I'm tired of walking in 5Ks."—Daniel Tosh

✳ A MAN FINISHES PUMPING GAS and goes into the store to pay. A sign on the pumps says, "Please tell cashier the pump number to pay." The man walks up to the counter and says to the clerk, "Number two." The clerk hands the man a set of keys, motions to a hallway next to the counter, and says "The second door on the left."

✳ IF YOU THINK NOBODY CARES you are alive, try missing a couple of payments.

✳ A CLEAR CONSCIENCE IS USUALLY the sign of a bad memory.

✳ A MAN GETS PULLED OVER by a police officer and his dog sniffs for drugs. The police officer goes over and says to the man, "My dog says you have weed in the car."

The man responds, "Well I don't know about that, but I want whatever got you talking to the dog!"

✳ TWO REDNECKS ARE WALKING ALONG when they see a dog licking his genitals. The first redneck says, "I wish I could do that."

The other responds, "If you tried he'd probably bite you."

✳ TWO MEN ARE FISHING WHEN the first man catches a very small fish. "This is going to be fantastic," the man says. "Wait until everyone sees this fish! Take a picture of me holding it."

The second man is confused by this excitement. "That fish isn't really that big," he tells his friend.

"It's not now," the man says, "but wait until I touch it up with Photoshop!"

✳ TWO NUNS ARE AT A traffic light when a man starts to squeegee their windshield. "I wish," says one of the nuns, "this man would leave us alone. We haven't got any money to give him." The man continues to wash their windows.

"Show him your cross," says the other nun. "Maybe he'll go away."

"Okay." The second nun rolls down the window and yells, "Go away, you bum!"

✳ WHAT DO YOU CALL SOMEONE who speaks three languages? Multilingual.

What do you call someone who speaks two languages? Bilingual.

What do you call someone who speaks one language? An American.

✳ WHAT DID THE TWO IPHONES say to the two iPads? "Want to get kinky and have a 4G?"

✳ WHY ARE TALL PEOPLE ALWAYS so well rested? They sleep longer in bed.

✳ WHAT DID THE HEAD OF the nudist colony say to the newest male members? "The first is always the hardest."

✳ DID YOU HEAR THE RUMOR about exit signs? They are on the way out.

✳ DID YOU HEAR ABOUT THE boy computer mouse that fell in love with the girl computer mouse? Friends say they clicked immediately.

✳ TWO TERRORISTS WERE ASSEMBLING LETTER bombs. After they completed one, the first terrorist said, "I don't think I put enough explosives in that one."

The second one said, "Well, open it up, and maybe add some more."

"But won't that make the device go off?" the first asked hesitantly.

"Don't be absurd," the second scolded, "the letter isn't addressed to you."

 ## Famous Funnies

"One of my college friends has a stutter and a lot of people think it's a bad thing, but to me it's just like starting certain words with a drum roll. That's not an impediment, that's suspense."—Demetri Martin

✳ A ROBBER CRASHES THROUGH THE doors of a deli, points a gun at the owner behind the counter, and screams, "Hand over the money or you're geography!"

The deli owner puts his hands up and says, "Don't you mean 'you'll be history'?"

The robber replies, "Don't change the subject!"

✳ HOW DID THE HIPSTER BURN his tongue? He tried to eat his food before it was cool.

✳ DID YOU KNOW 50 PERCENT of people use Google as a search engine and the other 50 percent use it to check to see if their Internet is connected?

 ## Famous Funnies

"There's no better feeling in the world than a warm pizza box on your lap."—Kevin James

✳ CHANGE YOUR FACEBOOK NAME TO Benefits so when someone adds you on Facebook, it will say, "You are now friends with Benefits."

✻ A MAN WAS EATING IN a restaurant when he desperately needed to pass gas. The music was really, really loud, so he timed his gas with the beat of the music. After a couple of songs, he started to feel better. He finished his coffee and noticed that everybody was staring at him. Then he suddenly remembered he was listening to his iPod.

✻ A WOMAN TELLS HER BEST friend, "Whenever I'm down in the dumps, I buy myself a dress, and it usually cheers me right up."

"That makes sense," her friend says, "because that's where I assumed you bought most of your clothes."

✻ A SOCIAL WORKER IS CONFRONTED by a mugger with a gun. "Your money or your life!" yells the mugger.

"You're out of luck, pal," the social worker answers. "I am a social worker, so I have no money and no life."

✻ WHAT DO YOU CALL AN epileptic in a vegetable garden? A seizure salad.

✻ A POLICEMAN CAME TO MY door yesterday and asked, "Where were you between four and six?"

So I said, "Probably either in kindergarten or first grade."

✻ DID YOU HEAR ABOUT THE woman who entered a contest to find the person with the most prominent veins in their legs? She didn't win, but she was varicose.

 Famous Funnies

"A day without sunshine is like, you know, night."—Steve Martin

✻ HOW DO YOU MAKE ANTIFREEZE? Steal her blankets.

✻ WHAT ARE THE THREE FASTEST forms of communication? Television, telephone, and tellawoman.

✳ WHAT DO YOU CALL A person who can't tell the difference between a ladle and spoon? Overweight.

✳ A WOMAN IS GETTING LUNCH ready when the phone rings. "This is the middle school calling about your son Phillip. He's been caught telling unbelievable lies."

"I'll say he has," the woman replies. "I don't have a son."

✳ HAVE YOU HEARD ABOUT THE new line of shampoos for hobos? It's called Go and Wash.

✳ A MAN BOUGHT A SELF-HELP book from the bookstore. The title of the book was *How to Handle Life's Biggest Disappointments*. When he opened the book to read it that night he realized all the pages were blank.

✳ DID YOU HEAR ABOUT THE man who received a life sentence just for one day of bobsleighing? He killed twenty Bobs in one day.

✳ A YOUNG MAN IS TRAVELING to work on the train. Without being able to control himself, he lets out an incredibly loud fart. Embarrassed, the man strikes up a conversation with the woman in the next seat.

"Do you happen to have today's paper?" the man asks.

"No, I don't," the woman says, "but I'm sure there is toilet paper in the train's restroom."

✳ TWO LONELY MEN ARE TALKING over lunch. The first guy says, "You wouldn't believe what happened this morning. A girl rode up to me on her bike, took off all her clothes, and said, 'Take whatever you want!' So I took the bike."

The second guy says, "Good choice. Her clothes probably wouldn't have fit you."

✳ A WOMAN HAD BEEN WALKING around Central Park for hours when she decided to sit down on a bench to rest her feet. A homeless man approached and said, "Well, it looks like my lucky night! I haven't made love to a woman in years."

"That's repulsive," the woman responded. "How dare you say such a thing?"

"Well, how do you expect me to react?" the homeless man responded. "You're sitting on my bed."

✱ DO YOU KNOW THE NAME of the man who invented the crossword puzzle? It begins with a P, then something, something, I, then something, H.

✱ A BRIDE IS GOING OVER the wedding planning with her mother. "I've got something new and something borrowed, but I don't have anything old or blue."

"Don't worry," the mother says, "your father's mother is coming and she hasn't paid her heating bill in months."

✱ DID YOU HEAR ABOUT THE new garlic and onions diet? You eat nothing but garlic and onions for a week. You don't lose much weight, but people will be standing so far away you'll appear smaller.

✱ "I SAW A RECENT PICTURE of you," a brother tells his sister who lives halfway around the world, "and I've got to be honest—you're looking kind of big."

"That's an awful thing to say!" the sister barks. "And where did you see a photo of me?" "Google Earth," the brother answers.

✱ WHY AREN'T THERE MANY FEMALE superheroes? Because by the time they got changed the world would be destroyed.

✱ THE CEO OF A MAJOR corporation is asked to give an address to shareholders at the yearly meeting. He asks the company press officer to write him a twenty-minute speech. When the CEO returns from the convention, he is furious at the press officer.

"Are you trying to kill my career?" the CEO barks. "I asked for a twenty-minute speech and you give me an hour-long speech. People were standing up and walking out."

"No," says the press officer, "I gave you exactly what you requested—a twenty-minute speech and two extra copies."

✳ A WOMAN WAS DRIVING IN rush hour traffic when the car in front of her stopped suddenly. She didn't have time to brake and smashed right into the car's back bumper. A dwarf got out of the driver's seat and approached the woman's car angrily. "I'm not happy!" the dwarf said through her closed window.

The woman rolled down the window and replied, "Good. My neck hurts, so I was hoping you were Doc."

✳ WHAT'S THE WORST PART ABOUT sitting in traffic? Getting run over.

✳ WHAT GOES *CLICK*, "HOW ABOUT now?" *click*, "How about now?" *click*, "How about now?"

A blind man attempting to solve a Rubik's Cube.

✳ A HANGOVER IS THE WRATH of grapes.

✳ FART IN CHURCH AND YOU'LL end up sitting in your own pew.

✳ WHILE WATCHING A MOVIE IN the theater, a man can't hear the dialogue over the chatter of the two women sitting in front of him. Unable to bear it any longer, he taps one of them on the shoulder. "Excuse me," he says, "I can't hear."

"I should hope not," one woman replies sharply. "This is a private conversation."

✳ A DRUNK MAN HAILS A taxi cab. When the taxi pulls over, the drunk sticks his head in the passenger side window and asks the driver, "Have you got room in here for a whole lobster and three bottles of wine?"

"Sure," replies the driver.

The drunk man says, "Fantastic!" and throws up on the passenger seat.

✳ A DRUNK MAN STARED AT a huge billboard for more than an hour. The billboard, advertising soda, wanted the world to Drink Canada Dry. So the drunk bought a bus ticket to give it a shot.

Ask the Comedian

Is there room for humor in the professional world?
There definitely is room for a little humor in the working world. Laughter alleviates stress and often works, when used sparingly, during long presentations or meetings. My only suggestion is to not gain the reputation of a person who jokes a little too much in the workplace. It could hinder your success.

✱ A LADY WALKS INTO A dress shop one afternoon after spotting a gorgeous strapless dress in the shop window. She tells the store clerk, "I'd like to try on that strapless dress in the window."

The store clerk replies, "You can try on the dress, Miss, but I think the changing room would be a much better place to do it."

✱ WHAT DO YOU GET WHEN you cross the Atlantic Ocean with the Titanic? About halfway.

✱ A NEW YORK MAN WAS forced to take a day off from work to appear for a minor traffic summons. He grew increasingly restless as he waited hour after endless hour for his case to be heard. When his name was called late in the afternoon, he stood before the judge, only to hear that court would be adjourned until the next day and he would have to return. "What for?" he snapped at the judge.

His Honor, equally irked by a tedious day and sharp query, roared, "Twenty dollars. Contempt of court. That's why!"

Then, noticing the man checking his wallet, the judge relented. "That's all right. You don't have to pay now."

The young man replied, "I'm just seeing if I have enough for two more words."

✱ THREE CONVICTS ESCAPE FROM JAIL and are being chased by police. They turn onto a dark alley and spot a bunch of potato sacks. Each of the three hides in one. A policeman quickly comes through the scene and hears a rustling from the potato sacks. He goes over to them and kicks the first potato sack.

"Meow!" says a convict. The policeman goes to the next one muttering, "Stupid cats."

He kicks the second potato sack and the second convict says, "Woof!"

"Stupid dogs!" says the policeman while moving on to the next potato sack. The policeman kicks it. Nothing happens. So he kicks it again and the last convict says, "Potato, potato!"

✸ A LADY ON A COMMUTER train is reading a newspaper article about life and death statistics.

Fascinated, she turns to the man next to her and asks, "Did you know that every time I breathe somebody dies?"

"Really?" he says. "Have you tried a good mouthwash?"

✸ A MAN IS DRIVING HOME, drunk as a skunk. Suddenly he has to swerve to avoid a tree, then another, then another. A police car pulls him over as he veers all over the road. The drunk tells the cop about all the trees in the road.

The cop says, "For God's sake! That's your pine tree air freshener swinging about."

✸ THERE IS A NEW PREACHER who wants to rent a house in the country. The only house available is rumored to be haunted. Since the preacher doesn't believe in such things, he rents it. It isn't long before the ghost makes its appearance. The preacher tells his friends about the ghost, but they don't believe him. They tell him the only way they would believe it is if he takes a picture of the ghost. The preacher goes home and calls for the ghost. When it appears, the preacher explains the situation and asks the ghost if it would mind having its picture taken. The ghost agrees. Days later, when the picture is developed, the ghost isn't visible. Feeling very disappointed, the preacher calls again for the ghost. When it appears, the preacher shows it the picture and wants to know why the ghost isn't in it. The ghost thinks a minute and replies, "Well, I guess the spirit was willing, but the flash was weak."

✳ TWO NEIGHBORS ARE OUT WORKING on their lawns when one man notices the other sprinkling a white powder around the perimeter of his property.

"Whatcha got there, pal?" the second man asks.

"Oh, this stuff?" the first replies. "This is lion repellent. It's supposed to keep all lions away."

"Lions?" The second man is baffled. "I've never seen or heard of any lion sightings within two hundred miles of here."

"I know," the man replies. "This stuff works great."

✳ TWO MUFFINS ARE BAKING IN an oven. One muffin turns to the other muffin and says, "Wow, it's really hot in here."

The other muffin says, "Oh my God! A talking muffin!"

✳ A MAN WALKS INTO A shoe store and tries on a pair of shoes.

"How do they feel?" asks the sales clerk. "They feel a little tight on my feet," replies the man. The assistant bends down and takes a closer look at the shoes and at the man's feet.

"Maybe try pulling the tongue out a little," the clerk says. "Sometimes that helps loosen things up."

"Okay," the man replies, "there, buth theyth sthill feelth a bith tighth."

✳ THREE MEN ARE CONVICTED OF a crime and sentenced to twenty years in solitary confinement. They're each allowed to bring something into the cell. The first man chooses as many books as can fit in the cell. The second man requests painting supplies. The last man requests twenty years' worth of cigarettes. On the morning of their release, the warden goes to visit each man in his cell.

The first man tells the warden, "These last twenty years of studying have been amazing. I'm going to go back to school and get my teaching degree."

The second man tells the warden, "I've become an accomplished artist and my works will hang in some of the most famous galleries in the world."

The warden enters the third man's cell and finds him surrounded by all of the cigarettes. The man tells the warden, "I probably should have also requested matches."

✱ JUST BEFORE BOARDING BEGAN, A flight attendant announced that the flight was overbooked. She explained that the airline was looking for volunteers to give up their seats. In exchange, the airline would offer a $100 voucher for the next flight and a First Class ticket for the plane leaving a few hours later. A small group of people ran up to the counter to take advantage of the offer. A few minutes later, all of the people returned to their seats with angry looks on their faces. The flight attendant got back on the intercom and announced, "If there is anyone besides the flight crew who'd like to volunteer, come up to the desk."

✱ ARNOLD AND HIS WIFE ARE cleaning out the attic one day when he comes across a ticket from the local shoe repair shop. The date stamped on the ticket shows that it is more than eleven years old. They both laugh and try to remember which of them might have forgotten to pick up a pair of shoes over a decade ago.

"Do you think the shoes will still be in the shop?" Arnold asks.

"Not very likely," his wife says.

"It's worth a try," Arnold says, pocketing the ticket. He goes downstairs, hops into the car, and drives to the store. With a straight face, he hands the ticket to the man behind the counter.

With a face just as straight, the man says, "Just a minute. I'll have to look for these." He disappears into a dark corner at the back of the shop. Two minutes later, the man calls out, "Here they are!"

"No kidding?" Arnold calls back. "That's terrific! Who would have thought they'd still be here after all this time?"

The man comes back to the counter, empty-handed. "They'll be ready Thursday," he says calmly.

* THE TOWN DRUNK STUMBLES OVER to a parking meter, stands in front of it, and reads that there are sixty minutes left until it expires.

"I don't believe it!" he cries out. "I've lost 100 pounds!"

* A PRISONER FINISHES A THIRTY-YEAR sentence and is released from jail. The moment he's outside the prison walls, he begins to jump up and down and scream out, "I'm free! I'm free!"

A little boy riding his bike past the prison grounds yells out to the ex-con, "Big deal! I'm four!"

* A MAN RELEASES A GENIE from a bottle and is granted only two wishes.

"Fine," says the man, "I can live with just two wishes. I'll take the best wine in the world and best woman in the world as my wife."

In a flash, the man has a bottle of the best wine money can buy. Unfortunately, he has to share it with his new wife, Mother Teresa.

* FIFTEEN MINUTES INTO A CROSS-COUNTRY flight, the plane's captain announces over the intercom, "Ladies and gentlemen, one of our engines has failed. There is nothing to worry about. Our flight will take an hour longer than scheduled, but we still have three engines left."

Thirty minutes later the captain announces, "Ladies and gentle-men, one more engine has failed and the flight will take an additional two hours. But don't worry. We can fly just fine on two engines."

An hour later the captain announces, "Ladies and gentlemen, one more engine has failed and our arrival will be delayed another three hours. But don't worry. We still have one engine left."

A young passenger turns to the man in the next seat and remarks, "If we lose one more engine, we'll be up here all day."

* A DRUNK MAN ARRIVES FOR his day in court. He appears before the judge, who looks down at his case file and says, "You've been brought here for drinking."

The drunk man smiles widely and says, "Great! Let's start the drinking!"

✱ AFTER A TWO-WEEK CRIMINAL TRIAL in a very high-profile bank robbery case, the jury finally ends its fourteen hours of deliberations and enters the courtroom to deliver its verdict to the judge. The judge turns to the jury foreman and asks, "Has the jury reached a verdict in this case?"

"Yes we have, Your Honor," the foreman responds.

"Would you please pass it to me," the judge declares, and motions for the bailiff to retrieve the verdict slip from the foreman and deliver it to him. After the judge reads the verdict himself, he delivers the verdict slip back to his bailiff to be returned to the foreman and instructs the foreman, "Please read your verdict to the court."

"We find the defendant not guilty of all four counts of bank robbery," states the foreman.

The family and friends of the defendant jump for joy at the sound of the "not guilty" verdict and hug each other as they shout expressions of gratitude. The defendant's attorney turns to his client and asks, "So, what do you think about that?"

The defendant looks around the courtroom slowly with a bewildered look on his face and then turns to his defense attorney and says, "I'm real confused here. Does this mean that I have to give all the money back?"

✱ A GUY WALKS INTO A bar and grabs a stool. Before he can order a drink, the bowl of pretzels on the bar in front of him says, "Hey, you're a handsome fellow."

The man tries to ignore the bowl of pretzels and orders a drink from the bartender. The bowl of pretzels tries to get the man's attention again by saying, "Ooh, a pilsner, that's a great choice. You seem like an incredibly smart man."

Getting very uncomfortable with the pretzel's comments, the guy says to the bartender, "Hey, what the heck is up with this bowl of pretzels? It just keeps saying really nice things about me."

The bartender says, "It's normal. The pretzels are complimentary."

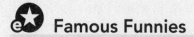 **Famous Funnies**

"To me, a lawyer is basically the person that knows the rules of the country. We're all throwing the dice, playing the game, moving our pieces around the board, but if there is a problem the lawyer is the only person who has read the inside of the top of the box."—Jerry Seinfeld

＊ TWO CLASSMATES ARE DISCUSSING THE current state of their alma mater at a reunion weekend barbecue. "Things have really gotten crazy here," the first man says. "Did you know the football coach makes three times the salary of the head of the English department?"

The second man responds, "Well that kind of makes sense. I'm pretty sure 100,000 screaming fans wouldn't show up on Saturday for a lecture on Shakespeare."

＊ A MAN WAKES UP ONE morning to find a gorilla on the roof of his house. He checks the yellow pages and finds an ad for "Gorilla Removers." He calls the number and the gorilla remover says he'll be over in thirty minutes. The gorilla remover arrives and gets out of his van with a ladder, a baseball bat, a shotgun, and a very nasty-looking pit bull.

"How does all this work?" the homeowner asks the gorilla remover.

"I'm going to put this ladder up against the roof. When I get up there I'm going to catch the gorilla off-guard and knock him off the roof with this baseball bat. When the gorilla falls off, the pit bull will grab the beast's testicles and not let go. The gorilla will then be subdued enough for me to put him in the cage in the back of the van."

The gorilla remover puts the ladder up against the house, grabs the bat and the shotgun, and walks toward the ladder. As he gets to the base of the ladder, he hands the shotgun to the homeowner.

"Why am I holding the shotgun?" asks the homeowner.

"If the gorilla knocks me off the roof, immediately shoot the pit bull."

✳ A YOUNG GIRL GETS SICK and her friend calls 911 for an ambulance. The operator asks where the house is.

"1419 Eucalyptus Street," the friend tells the 911 operator.

"All right, can you spell that for me?"

There is a long silence and the friend says, "How about I just drag her over to Oak Street and the ambulance meets us there?"

✳ LOOKING OUT INTO THE PITCH-BLACK night, a sea captain sees a light dead ahead. It's on a collision course with his ship.

He sends out a light signal: "Change your course ten degrees east."

The light signals back to the ship, "Change yours, ten degrees west."

Angrily, the captain sends a second signal, stating, "I'm a navy captain! Change your course, sir!"

"I'm a seaman, second class," comes back in reply. "You change your course, sir."

The captain is now furious. "I'm a battleship!" he signals. "I'm not changing course for anything."

He receives one final call, stating, "Well, I'm a lighthouse, so it's your call."

✳ A MAN WALKS INTO A bar and tells the bartender he'd like something tall, icy, and full of vodka. The bartender holds up his finger for the man to wait a minute and yells into the back room, "Hey Tiffany, someone is here looking for you!"

✳ A WOMAN CALLS HER HUSBAND'S cell phone to tell him the car is giving her a problem. She thinks there is water in the carburetor.

"How the heck would you know that?" the husband asks.

"Because I just drove it into a canal."

✳ A PASTOR WAS ENRAGED WHEN he found a bill for a $250 dress in his wife's purse. "How could you do this?" the pastor cried. "You know we're on an incredibly tight budget!"

"I know," the woman said, "but the devil himself was shopping with me. He convinced me the dress looked so good I had to buy it!"

The pastor consoled his wife with a hand on her shoulder. "In those moments, my love, you've got to yell out loud, 'Get behind me, Satan!'"

"I did that," the wife explained, "and he said, 'The dress even looks good from back here.'"

✳ DID YOU HEAR ABOUT THE social studies teacher fired for being cross-eyed? He couldn't control his pupils.

✳ A DRUNK MAN FALLS DOWN the front steps of the W Hotel in New York. He lands at the feet of a cab driver waiting for his next fare. The drunk man stands up and says, "Take me to the W Hotel!"

The cabby looks at the drunk man and tells him, "Buddy, you're at the W Hotel."

"Perfect," the man says, handing the driver a twenty-dollar bill, "but next time don't drive so fast."

✳ ONE EVENING AN OLD FARMER decides to go down to his pond. He hasn't been there in months, and feels the urge to check on things. As he gets closer, he hears loud giggling coming from the pond. He is shocked to find a bunch of young women skinny-dipping.

"Hey, what's going on here?" he shouts, alerting the women who are standing at the water's edge. All of the women scream in shock and swim to the deep end of the pond. One of the women shouts to the farmer, "We're not coming out until you leave, you pervert!"

The old man replies, "I didn't come down here to watch you ladies swim or see you naked! I'm here to feed the alligator!"

✳ A DIET GURU IS HOLDING a seminar in the conference room of a large hotel. "The food we eat," he explains, "is slowly killing us. Red meats attack the heart. Vegetables and fruits are sprayed with harmful pesticides. Even our drinking water is polluted! But do you know which food is much more dangerous than them all? Can anyone tell me what it is?"

A man in the back of the room raises his hand and, when called on, answers, "Wedding cake?"

✳ AFTER AN EXAMINATION OF A 4,000-year-old mummy, an archaeologist presents his findings to a group of his peers. "I can say beyond a shadow of a doubt that this man died of a heart attack." The group is stunned.

"How can you be so sure?" asks a fellow archaeologist. At that point, the archaeologist unrolls an old piece of paper for the group, which he found in the mummy's hand. It reads "$5,000 on Goliath."

 Famous Funnies

"I fantasize and idealize myself as Bugs Bunny, but I know deep down I'm Daffy Duck."—Patton Oswalt

✳ WHAT'S THE DIFFERENCE BETWEEN A vacuum cleaner and a Harley-Davidson owner? The position of the dirtbag.

✳ JILL DECIDES TO INTRODUCE HER elderly mother to the magic of the Internet. Her first move is to access Google. She tells her mother that the search engine can answer any question she has. Her mother is obviously skeptical.

"It's true, Mom," Jill says. "Think of something to ask and type it in that space."

Her mother sits with her fingers hovering above the keyboard, thinks for another minute, then types, "How is my cousin Helen doing?"

✳ A MAN IS DRIVING TO work when he notices the flash of a traffic camera. He figures that his picture has been taken for exceeding the limit, even though he knows that he wasn't speeding. Just to be sure, he circles the block and passes the exact same spot, driving even slower this time through. Again, the camera flashes. He thinks it is hilarious, since he is obviously doing nothing wrong, so he drives even slower as he passes through the light for a third time. The traffic camera takes his photo again. He does it a fourth and fifth time and is hysterical each time when the camera flash snaps his picture. The final time he passes through the light he is going 20 miles under the speed limit. Two weeks later, he gets five tickets in the mail for operating a car without a safety belt.

✳ VISITING A LOCAL CARNIVAL, DALE notices a fortuneteller and goes inside her tent. The room is very dark except for a glowing crystal ball in the center of a table. An old woman sits staring at the ball. She looks up when Dale enters.

"I will answer two questions," the old woman says, "for $100."

"One hundred dollars!" Dale balks. "Isn't that an obscene amount of money for this kind of service?"

"Yes it is," she responds. "You're down to one question."

✳ A MAN IS COMPLAINING ABOUT the local police to his neighbor.

"I'm sick of the cops in this town telling me how to drive when they are some of the worst drivers in the state."

"How do you know that?" the neighbor asks.

"Every week, I constantly pass signs on the side of the road that say *Police, Accident*."

✳ A YOUNG WOMAN GOES TO a fortuneteller. The fortuneteller tells her that she will be broke and unhappy until she turns fifty.

"What happens when I turn fifty?" the young woman asks, staring down at the cards.

"Oh nothing," says the fortuneteller. "You'll just be used to it by then."

✳ TWO COUNTRY BOYS FROM NORTH Carolina are sitting on the front porch drinking beer when a large truck hauling rolls and rolls of sod speeds by.

"I'm gonna do that when I win the lottery," says the first guy.

"Do what?" asks the second. "Drive a truck?"

"No, send my grass out to be mowed," he says.

✳ A COWBOY WALKS INTO A bar and orders a whiskey. As the barman's pouring the drink, the cowboy looks around him. "Where is everybody?" he asks.

"Gone to the hanging," says the barman.

"Hanging?" says the cowboy. "Who they hanging?"

"Brownpaper Pete," replies the barman.

"Brownpaper Pete? Why do they call him that?"

"Well," says the barman, "his hat's made of brown paper, his shirt's made of brown paper, his jacket's made of brown paper, and his trousers are made of brown paper."

"Really?" says the cowboy. "What they hanging him for?"

"Rustling."

✳ A WEALTHY LAWYER IS RIDING in his limousine when he sees two men along the side of the road eating grass. Disturbed, he orders his driver to stop and he gets out to investigate. He asks one man, "Why are you eating grass?"

"We don't have any money for food," the poor man replies. "We have to eat grass."

"Well then, you can come with me to my house and I'll feed you," the lawyer says.

"But sir, I have a wife and two children with me. They are over there, under that tree."

"Bring them along," the lawyer replies. Turning to the other poor man he says, "You come with us also."

The second man, in a pitiful voice, then says, "But sir, I also have a wife plus six children with me!"

"Bring them all, as well," the lawyer answers. They all enter the car, which is no easy task, even for a car as large as the limousine. Once under way, one of the poor fellows turns to the lawyer and says, "Sir, you are too kind. Thank you for taking all of us with you."

The lawyer replies, "Glad to do it. You'll really love my place; the grass is almost a foot high!"

＊ THERE ARE ONLY TWO KINDS of people in the world. There are those who wake up in the morning and say, "Good morning, Lord," and there are those who wake up in the morning and say, "Good Lord, it's morning."

＊ A COMPLETELY INEBRIATED MAN IS stumbling down the street with one foot on the curb and one foot in the gutter. A cop pulls up and says, "I've got to take you in, pal. You're obviously drunk."

The drunk says, "Officer, are you absolutely sure I'm drunk?"

"Yeah buddy, I'm sure," says the cop. "Let's go."

Breathing a sigh of relief, the wino says, "Thank goodness. I thought I was crippled."

＊ A MAN SPENDS THE ENTIRE night getting hammered at his local pub. After last call, the man stands up from his stool but falls flat on his face trying to walk. He pulls himself up in the doorway of the bar, attempts to stand, but falls flat on his face to the sidewalk. He drags himself to his car and drives home. He tries to unlock his front door, finally gets it unlocked, but falls flat on his face in the hallway of his home. His wife is standing on the steps to the bedroom, waiting for the man. "You've been out drinking again, haven't you?"

"What makes you say that?" the man asks, still lying on the cold wooden floor.

"Because the bar called. You forgot your wheelchair again!"

✱ GEORGE IS JUST ABOUT TO go to bed when his wife tells him that he's left the light on in the garden shed, which she can see from the bedroom window. George opens the back door to go turn off the light, but sees that there are people in the shed stealing things. He phones the police, who ask, "Is someone in your house?" George says no. Then they say that all patrols are busy, and that he should simply lock his door and an officer will be along when available.

George says, "Okay," hangs up, counts to thirty, and phones the police again.

"Hello. I just called you a few seconds ago because there are people in my shed. Well, you don't have to worry about them now because I've just shot all the sons of bitches!" Then he hangs up. Within five minutes, three police cars, an Armed Response unit, and an ambulance show up at George's residence.

The police catch the burglars red-handed. One of the policemen says to George, "I thought you said that you'd shot them!"

George says, "I thought you said there was nobody available."

✱ A JUDGE ASKS A DEFENDANT to please stand.

"You are charged with murdering a garbage man with a chain saw."

From the back of the courtroom, a man shouts, "You liar!"

"Silence in the court!" The judge turns to the defendant again and says, "You are also charged with killing a paperboy with a shovel."

"You tightwad!" blurts the spectator.

"Quiet!" yells the judge. "You are also charged with killing a mailman with an electric drill."

"You cheap son of a . . ." the spectator starts to shout.

The judge thunders back, "I will hold you in contempt! What is the reason for your outbursts?"

"I've lived next to that liar for ten years now," the man explains, "but do you think he ever had a tool when I needed to borrow one?"

* HAVE YOU SEEN THE NEW website for sufferers of conjunctivitis? It's a site for sore eyes.

* A GUY WALKS INTO A bar and asks for a pint of less.

"Less?" the bartender asks. "What the heck is less?"

"No clue," the man answers. "My doctor just told me to drink less."

* THE LEADER OF THE VEGETARIAN society just couldn't control himself anymore. He needed to try some pork, just to see what it tasted like. So one summer day he told his members he was going on a vacation. He traveled to a town in a neighboring state, and headed to the nearest restaurant. After sitting down, he ordered a roasted pig, and impatiently waited for his delicacy. After just a few minutes, he heard someone call his name, and to his great chagrin he saw one of his fellow members walking toward him. Just at that same moment, the waiter walked over with a huge platter, holding a full roasted pig with an apple in its mouth.

"Isn't that something," said the leader after only a moment's pause. "All I do is order an apple, and look what it comes with!"

CHAPTER 11

Classic Jokes

Everyone loves a classic joke: A priest and a rabbi get together. A guy goes into a bar. A blonde does . . . anything. Three simple premises that kick off some of the funniest jokes of all time. These following jokes are the classics that will never get old, including kid-friendly comedic staples like knock-knock jokes and one-liners.

Guy Walks Into a Bar . . .

✱ A GUY WALKS INTO A bar and drunkenly yells at the bartender, "I slept with your mother!"

The bartender yells back, "Dad, you're drunk again, go home!"

✱ A GUY WALKS INTO A bar and orders ten shots of tequila. The guy starts slamming the shots back one after the other.

Bartender says, "Hey, slow down, buddy!"

The guy says, "No way! If you had what I have you'd be drinking this fast too."

The bartender says, "Oh, I'm sorry. I didn't know. What have you got?"

The guy takes another shot and says, "Oh, about seventy-five cents."

✷ A GUY WALKS INTO A bar with a dog under his arm. He announces to everyone in the bar that his dog can talk and he will make a $1,000 bet with anyone who doesn't believe him. The bartender sees this as a great opportunity, so he takes the man up on the wager. The man looks at the dog and says, "What is the top of a house called?"

The dog says, "Roof."

Quite annoyed, the bartender vents his grief in defeat. "Well, how about a different word, double or nothing?" the man says.

The bartender begrudgingly accepts as the man asks the dog, "Who was the greatest baseball player ever?"

In a muffled response the dog says, "Ruth." Furious, the bartender grabs the man and the dog and throws them out of the bar.

As they land on the sidewalk, the dog looks at the man with a puzzled look and says, "DiMaggio?"

 Famous Funnies

"When I woke up this morning my girlfriend asked me, 'Did you sleep good?' I said, 'No, I made a few mistakes.'"—Steven Wright

A Priest and a Rabbi . . .

✷ A PRIEST AND A RABBI strike up a friendly conversation and after a while, the priest asks the rabbi, "Tell me, did you ever, in a moment of weakness, partake in the eating of bacon?"

The rabbi says, "Yes. I was staying at a motel where no one knew me and it was on the breakfast buffet."

The priest nods, empathetically. The rabbi then asks the priest a question.

"Did you ever . . . you know . . . sleep with a woman?"

The priest replies, "Yes, in a period of weakness during my first year in seminary. I met a young woman at a cafe and one thing led to another and, well, yes. We made love."

"I see." The rabbi nods, knowingly, before adding, "It's way better than bacon, isn't it?"

✳ A PRIEST AND A RABBI have a fender-bender in the middle of an intersection. They both get out of their cars to survey the damage. The rabbi turns to the priest and says, "You know, this is a pretty trivial event, all things considered. I've got some Manischewitz in the car—how about you and I drink to the friendship between our two faiths?" The priest readily agrees, and takes a big swig from the bottle the rabbi offers. Then the rabbi puts the cork back in and tosses the bottle in his car.

"Aren't you going to drink to your own toast?" the priest asks, puzzled.

"Oh," the rabbi responds, "I think I'll wait until after the cops leave."

 Famous Funnies

> "If truth is beauty, how come no one has their hair done in the library?"—Lily Tomlin

✳ A PRIEST, A RABBI, AND a pastor are sitting at a bar. They are arguing over who is the best at what they do. They decide that to prove who is the best, each will go into the woods on his own and convert a bear to his religion. A week later, they are again at the bar. The priest says, "I saw a bear by the river and started talking to him about the Lord's word. He liked it so much that he now comes to Mass every week."

The pastor says, "Well, I found a bear in a clearing. I started reading the Bible to him. He loved it so much that he is now going to be baptized in about a week."

The priest and the pastor turn to the rabbi, who has a broken arm, several bruises, and is wearing a neck collar. He says, "You know what, looking back, maybe I shouldn't have started with circumcision."

✻ A PRIEST, A RABBI, AND a minister are fishing in a boat. The priest says, "I'm thirsty. I'm going to the shore to get something to drink." So he walks across the water to the shore, gets a soda, walks back across the water, and gets back in the boat.

A little while later, the minister says, "I'm thirsty. I'm going to the shore to get something to drink." So the minister gets up, walks to the shore, gets a soda, and walks back, just like the priest did.

The rabbi thinks to himself, "Hey, that's pretty cool. I think I'll try it." So the rabbi gets up, saying, "I'm thirsty. I'm going to the shore to get something to drink." So he steps out of the boat and drowns.

Then the priest says to the minister, "Do you think we should have told him about the rocks?"

Blondes

✻ A BLONDE GOES TO AN electronics store, walks up to the sales associate, and says, "I would like to buy the TV in the corner."

The associate says, "Sorry ma'am, we don't serve blondes."

Furious, the blonde goes home and dyes her hair black. The next day, she returns to the store. She sees the same associate and says, "I would like to buy the TV in the corner."

He replies, "Sorry ma'am, we don't serve blondes here."

Figuring the associate recognized her, the woman goes home and this time dyes her hair red. She returns to the store the following day. The previous associate isn't there, and she tells another associate, "I would like to purchase the TV in the corner."

The associate says, "Sorry ma'am, we don't serve blondes here."

The blonde says, "You have never seen me before. How do you know I'm blonde?"

He responds, "That is not a TV. It's a microwave!"

 Famous Funnies

> "My fake plants died because I did not pretend to water them."—Mitch Hedberg

✳ A BLONDE WENT TO A football game with her boyfriend. They had great seats right behind their team's bench. After the game, he asked her how she liked the experience.

"Oh, I really liked it," she replied, "especially the tight pants and all the big muscles, but I just couldn't understand why they were killing each other over twenty-five cents."

Dumbfounded, her date asked, "What do you mean?"

"Well, they flipped a coin, one team got it, and then for the rest of the game, all they kept screaming was, 'Get the quarterback! Get the quarterback!' I'm like, hello? It's only twenty-five cents!"

✳ WHY WON'T BLONDES TAKE THEIR iPhones to the bathroom? They don't want to give away their IP address!

✳ A BLONDE GOES TO THE doctor and asks for help with losing weight. The doctor figures he should make it as simple for her as possible, so he tells her to eat normally for two days, then skip a day, eat normally for two days, then skip a day, etc. The blonde says she will try it and will come back in two weeks. Two weeks later, the blonde shows up at the doctor's office ten pounds lighter. The doctor is surprised she lost so much weight and asks her how it went. The blonde says the first week was really tough.

The doctor asks, "Was it the fasting?"

The blonde answers, "No, it was all the skipping."

* A BLONDE GOES TO HER gynecologist and tells the doctor that no matter how hard she and her husband have tried, she just can't get pregnant.

The doctor says, "Okay, take off your clothes and lie down on the table."

The blonde says, "Um, all right. But I was really hoping to have my husband's baby."

 ## Comedy Facts

While there is no "funniest joke ever," the term "The Funniest Joke in the World" is the title most frequently used for a *Monty Python's Flying Circus* comedy sketch. The premise of the sketch is that one joke is so funny that anyone who reads or hears the joke promptly dies from laughter. The sketch appeared in the first episode of the television show *Monty Python's Flying Circus* on October 5, 1969. The sketch was later re-created in a shorter version for the movie *And Now for Something Completely Different*.

* A BLONDE WOMAN IS SPEEDING down the road in her little red sports car and is pulled over by a female police officer, who is also a blonde. The officer asks to see the lady's driver's license. The woman digs through her purse and gets progressively more agitated.

"What does it look like?" she finally asks.

The policewoman replies, "It's square and it has your picture on it."

The driver finally finds a mirror in her purse, looks at it, and hands it to the policewoman. "Here it is," she says.

The officer looks at the mirror and then hands it back, saying, "Okay, you can go. I didn't realize you were a cop."

Comedy Facts

Many famous actors and actresses have tried their hand at stand-up comedy before embarking on a career in acting. Ron Perlman, Emma Thompson, Michael Keaton, and Steve Buscemi all gave stand-up comedy a shot before moving on to bigger and better roles.

✱ A BLONDE GOES TO SEE a ventriloquist act. All is well until half-way through, when the ventriloquist makes a blonde joke. The blonde stands up.

"That is very offensive, to judge people on how they look! You owe me, and every blonde in the room, an apology!"

The ventriloquist apologizes profusely. "I'm so sorry, I didn't mean to offend you."

"Shut up, you! I was talking to the little jerk sitting on your knee!"

✱ A BLONDE WALKS INTO A bar holding a handful of dog poop. She shows it to the bartender and says, "Today is my lucky day! I almost stepped in this outside."

✱ A BLONDE GOES TO THE blood bank to make a donation. The nurse asks her, "What type are you?"

The blonde quickly responds, "I'm an outgoing cat-lover."

✱ TWO BLONDES ARE ATTEMPTING TO unlock their car with a coat hanger. They locked their keys inside before going in the mall. "I don't think this is going to work," the first blonde says, attempting to get the hanger near the lock.

"It better work," says the second blonde. "It's starting to rain and the top is down."

✱ A BLONDE IS EATING A Tootsie Roll Pop on a park bench. An interested young man approaches and asks her, "So, how many licks does it take to get to the center of a Tootsie Roll Pop?"

Without a thought the blonde replies, "I'm not sure, but it took almost the whole day just to lick through the wrapper."

 Famous Funnies

"Racism isn't born, folks, it's taught. I have a two-year-old son. You know what he hates? Naps! End of list."—Denis Leary

✱ A MAN COMES HOME ONE night to find his blonde wife reading his personal journal.

"I can explain everything," he begins.

She interrupts him mid-sentence and exclaims, "You're darn right you've got some explaining to do, and you can start with telling me who April, May, and June are!"

100 Jokes for Young Folks

1. Which haircut do sea captains hate the most? Crew cuts.
2. Why can't a bicycle stand on its own? Because it's two-tired.
3. What happened when the piano fell down the mine shaft? It caused a few flat miners.
4. What do you call a fake noodle? An impasta!
5. What do you call a pig with a black belt in karate? A pork chop!
6. How do you know when a clock is hungry? It goes back four seconds.
7. Did you hear about the man who bumped his head on the upholstery machine? He's fully recovered.

8. What do you call a person who listens to both sides of an argument? A neighbor.

9. Seagulls fly over the sea, but what type of bird flies over the bay? A bagel.

10. What did the belly button say before he left the room? I'm outtie here.

11. How is a computer like a grandparent? The first thing that goes on both is their memory.

12. What happened when the computer fell off the desk? It slipped a disk.

13. What do you call a sleeping bull? A bull-dozer.

14. Why aren't teddy bears ever hungry? They are always stuffed!

15. Why did the turkey cross the road? To prove he was no chicken.

16. Which animal has even more lives than a cat? Frogs; they croak all the time.

17. What is black, white, green, and bumpy? A pickle in a tuxedo.

18. What kind of nuts get sick the most? Cashews!

19. What is black and white and black and white and black and white? A penguin falling down the stairs.

20. Why are barbers never allowed to run races? They know too many short cuts.

21. How do you make a tissue dance? You put a little boogie in it.

22. What kind of shoes can you make out of bananas? Slippers.

23. What type of music scares balloons? Pop music.

24. What goes up and down all day but never moves? A flight of stairs.

25. What did the piece of paper say to the pen? Write on!

26. Why was the broom late for work? It over swept.

27. What kind of car does Mickey Mouse's girlfriend drive? A Minnie van.

28. What does a hat become when you drop it into the Atlantic Ocean? Wet.

29. What kind of lights did Noah have on the Ark? Flood lights.

30. What do you call a very young army? An infantry.

31. Why did the TV jump in front of the truck? To be a flat screen.

32. What did the ground say to the earthquake? You really crack me up.

33. Why did the nose hate school? He was always getting picked on.

34. What kind of bait do librarians use for fishing? Bookworms.

35. Why doesn't the sun have to go to college? Because it already has a million degrees.

36. What do lawyers wear to court? Lawsuits.

37. What's another name for a happy cowboy? A jolly rancher.

38. What do you call a boomerang that doesn't work? A stick.

39. What do cheerleaders eat for breakfast before the big game? Cheerios.

40. Why didn't anyone want the pig on their basketball team? He was a real ball hog.

41. What is harder to catch the faster you run? Your breath.

42. What is the hardest part about skydiving? The ground.

43. What subject are witches always the best at in school? Spelling.

44. Why did the baker stop making doughnuts? He got sick of the hole business.

45. Which nails do carpenters hate to hit with their hammers? Fingernails.

46. What do you call a chicken at the North Pole? Lost.

47. Why was Cinderella thrown off the basketball team? She ran away from the ball.

48. Why did the mechanic sleep under cars? To go to work oily in the morning.

49. What did the caveman call the blind dinosaur? I-don't-think-he-saurus.

50. Why did Tigger stick his head in the toilet? He was looking for Pooh.

51. Why do fish make terrible tennis partners? They don't like to play near the net.

52. What do you call cheese that doesn't belong to you? Nacho cheese.

53. What's a vampire's favorite sport? Batminton.

54. Why didn't the skeleton go to his senior prom? He had no body to go with.

55. What sickness did everyone on *Star Trek* get? The chicken spocks.

56. What is purple and 5,000 miles long? The Grape Wall of China.

57. Where can you find a turtle with no feet? Exactly where you last left him.

58. What does Thor wear under his costume? Thunderwear.

59. How do angels greet each other in heaven? They say halo.

60. Which professional sports team never uses cash? The Chargers.

61. Why was the scarecrow given a promotion? He was outstanding in his field.

62. What photo do Santa's helpers love to take? Elfies.

63. Where did the chess piece sell his old furniture? The pawn shop.

64. What do you get if you print out all your cell phone messages? A textbook.

65. What kind of paint do shark artists use? Watercolors.

66. Where do retired sailors shop? Old Navy.

67. What happened when the Dutch boy tried to flush his shoe down the toilet? He got a clog.

68. What happened when the zoo ran out of bamboo to eat? Panda-monium.

69. Why couldn't the frog find his car? It got toad away.

70. Why wouldn't Times New Roman go out with Comic Sans? He wasn't her type.

71. How does Darth Vader get out of work? He calls in Sith.

72. Which Chinese food item weighs the most? One-ton soup.

73. Who is constantly bossing around the office supplies? The ruler.

74. What game is popular at dentist sleepovers? Tooth or dare.

75. What does Justin Bieber do on weekends to make extra money? He Baby Baby Babysits.

76. Where do archers do all their shopping? Target.

77. What do you call a cow with no legs? Ground beef.

78. Did you hear the joke about the toilet? I can't tell it because it's too dirty.

79. Which dinosaur knows the most words? The thesaurus.

80. How do you get an astronaut baby to sleep? Rocket.

81. What kind of car does Luke Skywalker drive? A Toy-Yoda.

82. How do you serve smart hamburgers? On honor rolls.

83. What do you call a fairy who hates bathing? A stinker bell.

84. Where does a boat go when it catches a cold? The dock.

85. Why can't a tyrannosaurus clap? It's extinct.

86. Why did the fast cat get suspended from school? For being a cheetah.

87. What does a piece of toast wear to bed? Jam-mies.

88. Why did the orange lose the race? He ran out of juice.

89. Why didn't the skeleton try stand-up comedy? He didn't have the guts.

90. Why did the tomato turn red? It saw the salad dressing.

91. How do you make a hot dog stand? Take away its chair.

92. What happens to racecar drivers when they overeat? They get Indy-gestion.

93. Why did the invisible man turn down a job? He just couldn't see himself doing it.

94. What do you get when you cross a pig and a centipede? Bacon and legs.

95. What do butter and jelly do around the campfire? They tell toast stories.

96. What did the duck say when it bought ChapStick at the pharmacy? "Put it on my bill."

97. What does a baby computer call his father? Data!

98. How did the computer catch a cold? Its owner left its Windows open.

99. What do you call a camel with no humps? Humphrey.

100. Why does a chicken coop only have two doors? Because if it had four, it would be a chicken sedan.

A Classic Collection of Knock-Knock Jokes

Knock! Knock!
Who's there?
Ho-ho.
Ho-ho who?
You know, your Santa impression could use a little work.

Knock! Knock!
Who's there?
Hanna.
Hanna who?
Hanna partridge in a pear tree!

Knock! Knock!
Who's there?
Cash.
Cash who?

No thanks, but I would like a peanut instead!

Knock! Knock!
Who's there?
Doris.
Doris who?
Doris locked, that's why I'm knocking!

Knock! Knock!
Who's there?
Interrupting cow.
Interrup-
Mooooooooooooooo!

Knock! Knock!
Who's there?
Honey bee.
Honey bee who?
Honey bee a dear and get me the remote.

Knock! Knock!
Who's there?
Madam.
Madam who?
Madam foot got caught in the door!

Knock! Knock!
Who's there?
Me.
Me who?
No, seriously, it's just me. I am telling a knock-knock joke.

 **Famous Funnies**

"Did you ever see the customers in health food stores? They are pale, skinny people who look half dead. In a steak house, you see robust, ruddy people. They're dying, of course, but they look terrific."—Bill Cosby

Knock! Knock!
Who's there?
Owls.
Owls who?
That's correct, owls who!

Knock! Knock!
Who's there?
Cows go.
Cows go who?
No, cows go moo!

Knock! Knock!
Who's there?
Echo.
Echo who?
Echo who? Echo who?

Knock! Knock!
Who's there?
Oink oink.
Oink oink who?
Make up your mind, are you a pig or an owl?!

Knock! Knock!
Who's there?
Ya.
Ya who?
What are you so excited about?

Knock! Knock!
Who's there?
Broken pencil.
Broken pencil who?
Oh, never mind, it's pointless!

APPENDIX A

Comedy Websites

Bad Slava

www.badslava.com

Open mics are essential for any aspiring comic. Bad Slava is the world's largest open mic website, dedicated to listing the best open mic opportunities across the United States and the world.

College Humor

www.collegehumor.com

Founded by two high school friends, College Humor delivers daily humorous content, including videos, pictures, articles, and jokes.

The Comedy Soapbox

www.comedysoapbox.com

Since 2003, The Comedy Soapbox has evolved from a simple website for an independent comedy room into the largest comedy community on the Internet. The company was founded by comedians and for comedians with the purpose of helping working comics increase the opportunities for living the dream of a career in stand-up and for developing the art of stand-up comedy.

Funny or Die

www.funnyordie.com

Funny or Die is a comedy video website founded by Will Ferrell and Adam McKay's production company, Gary Sanchez Productions. The website contains original and user-generated content. Funny or Die contains exclusive material from numerous famous contributors and also has its own Funny or Die Team, which creates original daily material for the site.

Laughspin

www.laughspin.com

Founded as *Punchline Magazine* in 2005, Laughspin's goal is to provide the best comedy news, videos, interviews, and opinion in an easily accessible, highly functional package online.

The Onion

www.theonion.com

"America's Finest News Source," the Onion is an entertainment site featuring satirical articles reporting on international, national, and local news.

Reader's Digest

www.rd.com/submit-joke

Reader's Digest is not only a great research site for humorous stories, but it also accepts jokes, real-life tales, and themed submissions for its magazine and website. If the submitted material is chosen for publication, the company will even pay $100.

Splitsider

www.splitsider.com

Splitsider is a website about comedy and the people who create it. It covers movies, TV shows, web videos, books, and any other format and takes an insider's look at the world of comedy.

Stage Time Magazine

www.stagetimemagazine.com

Stage Time is an online magazine covering the craft and business of stand-up comedy. Launched in 2005, Stage Time is one of the leading media resources for comedians and provides informative interviews, career advice articles, and insightful commentary from some of the top comedic minds in the business.

APPENDIX B

Books about Humor, Comedy, and Writing

And Here's the Kicker: Conversations with 21 Top Humor Writers on Their Craft, **by Mike Sacks**

In this fascinating and entertaining collection, twenty-one of the top humor writers of the past fifty years discuss the comedy-writing process, their influences, their experiences in the industry, and what exactly happens to make something funny. Author David Sedaris, Paul Feig (co-creator of *Freaks and Geeks*), Ricky Gervais, and Sacha Baron Cohen are just some of the famous funny people who share stories of humor and humanity.

The Comedy Bible: From Stand-Up to Sitcom—The Comedy Writer's Ultimate "How To" Guide, **by Judy Carter**

With the word "bible" in the title, it's obvious this book is an authority on all things comedy. Written by comedy coach, author, and speaker Judy Carter, *The Comedy Bible* breaks down all things funny—from how to develop a stand-up routine to the essentials for writing a spec script.

Comedy Writing Secrets: The Best-Selling Book on How to Think Funny, Write Funny, Act Funny, and Get Paid for It, **by Mel Helitzer and Mark Shatz**

This step-by-step guide on how to turn your comedic talents into a profitable career is now in its second edition. Written by authors Shatz, a former stand-up, and Helitzer, once named "the funniest professor in the country" by *Rolling Stone* magazine, *Comedy Writing Secrets* offers tips and tricks on writing humor for specific markets and forms including editorials, the Internet, columns, speeches, advertising, greeting cards, and even promotional materials.

I'm Dying Up Here: Heartbreak and High Times in Stand-Up Comedy's Golden Era, **by William Knoedelseder**

Veteran reporter William Knoedelseder was assigned by the *Los Angeles Times* to cover the city's burgeoning comedy scene in the mid-1970s. Among the fresh faces of stand-up that Knoedelseder spoke to were David Letterman, Andy Kaufman, Jay Leno, Robin Williams, and Richard Lewis. *I'm Dying Up Here* highlights the vicious labor dispute between the stand-ups and the owner of the Comedy Store in Los Angeles, who refused to pay comics while turning a profit on their work. The book is a biography of some of the biggest stars of a generation and a look into the life of the struggling comic.

Comedic Biographies and Autobiographies

Making people laugh is tough business. If the opportunity ever arises, ask any of the following comedy legends if this is true. They'll say yes, even if the answer comes out as a joke. Here are some fascinating books written by and about some of the most influential funny people of the last fifty years. While these books won't necessarily explain the crafting of a joke, they will provide an inside look at the business of making strangers laugh.

Born Standing Up: A Comic's Life, by Steve Martin

In the early 1970s, Steve Martin exploded onto the comedy scene. By 1978, Martin was the biggest concert draw in the history of stand-up, selling out venues across the country. He was on television, in popular movies, and was the undisputed king of stand-up during this time. In 1981, at the height of his popularity, he quit stand-up forever. *Born Standing Up: A Comic's Life* is the story of his rise to the top, his life in front of the microphone, why he did stand-up, and why he walked away.

Bossy Pants, by Tina Fey

Fey, once an awkward young girl with a dream of performing, tells the story of her comedy beginnings, her early days in the Chicago Improv scene, her stint as head writer for *Saturday Night Live*, and all of the crazy moments in between. *Bossy Pants* is a candid look at the reigning queen of sketch comedy.

I Didn't Ask to Be Born (But I'm Glad I Was), by Bill Cosby

The legendary comedian, author, and activist is as relevant now as he was when he debuted in comedy clubs almost forty years ago. He has sold more record albums than any other comedian in history. One of the most influential performers and comedic voices of the second half of the twentieth century, Cosby's comedy has conquered every form of media. This book provides a candid peek into the mind of "The Cos."

Love All the People: The Essential Bill Hicks, by Bill Hicks

Not quite the typical biography, *Love All the People: The Essential Bill Hicks* is a collection of transcribed stand-up acts, journal entries, interviews, and essays by a prolific comedian and genius mind who never really had his moment in the spotlight. Hicks's life was cut short at the age of thirty-two. The book traces his evolution from a brilliant stand-up to a comic speaking without fear.

***The Trials of Lenny Bruce: The Rise and Fall of an American Icon*, by Ronald Collins and David Skover**
Lenny Bruce's fight for the first amendment right to freedom of speech is one of the reasons comedians are allowed to explore formerly taboo topics on stage. This book is an oral history of Bruce's fight, on stage and in courtrooms across the United States, and a glimpse into a comic genius and genuinely tortured soul.

INDEX

We Have EVERYTHING on Anything!

The Everything® list spans a wide range of subjects, with more than 500 titles covering 25 different categories:

Business	History	Reference
Careers	Home Improvement	Religion
Children's Storybooks	Everything Kids	Self-Help
Computers	Languages	Sports & Fitness
Cooking	Music	Travel
Crafts and Hobbies	New Age	Wedding
Education/Schools	Parenting	Writing
Games and Puzzles	Personal Finance	
Health	Pets	